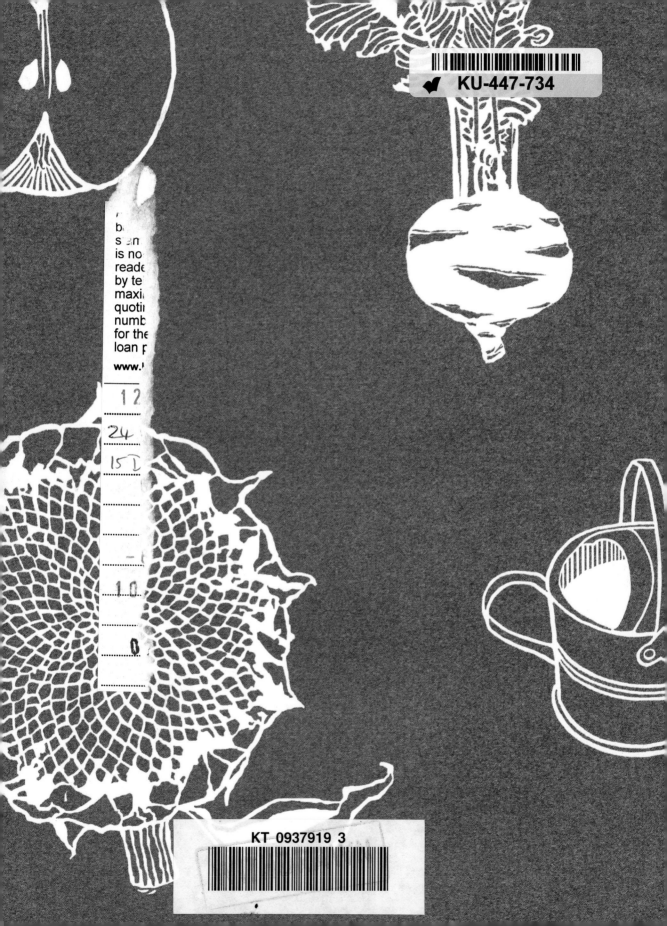

THE EDIBLE GARDEN

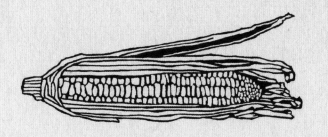

THE EDIBLE GARDEN

How to have your garden and eat it

ALYS FOWLER

BBC BOOKS   Gardeners' World

FOR JULIET

(This book is dedicated to Juliet Glaves)

Alys Fowler

Alys trained at the Horticultural Society, the New York Botanical Garden and the Royal Botanic Garden at Kew. After finishing her training, she worked as a journalist for the trade magazine, *Horticulture Week*, and then joined the *Gardeners' World* team as a horticultural researcher. The lure of the garden, however, proved too much and in 2006 Alys became Head Gardener at Berryfields. She is now a permanent presenter from Greenacre, the show's new home. Alys's inspiration for urban gardening comes from her time volunteering in a community garden on the Lower East Side in Manhattan, New York City. Much of the ethic, thrift and spirit she encountered there is found in her work today.

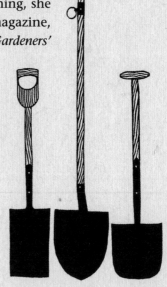

CONTENTS

Introduction — 6

PART 1: THINGS TO KNOW — 14
The New Order — 16
Growing Healthy Plants — 34
Getting Your Garden Started — 46

PART 2: THINGS TO GROW — 58
Everything Essential That I Know
About Growing Vegetables
(and Flowers) — 60
The Edible Directory — 72
Flowers — 166
Seed Saving — 186

PART 3: REAPING YOUR HARVEST — 194
Harvesting — 196
Home Cooking — 218
Brews — 240

Resources — 250
Index — 252
Acknowledgements — 252

Introduction

I want it all, the whole far-flung earth and everything in it.

I want streams and hills, rivers and seas, mountains and pastures. I want a whole, happy, earth. And when I'm not being overly ambitious about my environmental desires, I also want a garden with a little bit of everything in it. These two desires are not unconnected, my happy earth will, in part (and no small part), be by my ability to grow a large percentage of my food in my garden, in a way that does not devour resources.

It has never been possible for us all to have gardens big enough for herbaceous borders, rockeries, orchards and vegetable patches. And it is not going to happen now, but too often I hear the same complaint, 'I want to grow vegetables but my garden isn't big enough for a separate patch'. To this I say mix it together and don't worry about the rules that say things need to be segregated. You can have your vegetables, fruit and flowers in a productive garden that is beautiful to look at. It is actually not difficult to marry the joys of growing your own with the beauty of a flower garden.

There are thousands of us out there that are desperate for wholesome, home-grown food, but not at the expense of our city lives. This book is about taking the good life and re-fashioning it on bits of wasteland, in back gardens and on fire escapes. From planting plans to political issues, this book looks at how and why we need to make our gardens more productive. In today's world, growing your own not only makes economic sense, it's a powerful political gesture about our oil-reliant food chain and how we can go about fixing it.

Whether you have a balcony, a courtyard or a sprawling plot this is about saying that your garden pleases you, pleases your palette and pleases the wider environment.

A LITTLE HISTORY

Growing in straight lines hasn't always been the norm for vegetable gardens, nor have they been exclusively about vegetables. The segregated kitchen or productive garden is a Victorian throwback, it says more about

money and space than anything else. While the rich kept their vegetables, flowers and ornamental plants strictly separated, smaller gardens elsewhere were more likely to be a mixture of both.

The traditional cottage garden is a mixture of flowers and vegetables, often grown in what might appear to be a slightly haphazard manner. The potager is a grander version, with more order (and more lines), but is essentially about mixing the benefits of flowers, fruits and vegetables together. The cottage garden is quintessentially English, the potager says France, and if you hop across the pond you'll find another, more contemporary, style called edible landscaping. Edible landscaping aims to create a space in which useful plants are designed into the garden landscape. In other words, you can eat your view.

Although some edible landscapes can be quite formal (using vegetables like bedding plants to create careful patterns), others happily abandon traditional formalities and seem to mix form, function and frivolity. They may include herbs for the kitchen, cut flowers for the vase, plants to bring in beneficial insects, vegetables to dine off, and maybe habitat nooks such as ponds and insects' homes to bring the rest of nature in to play.

It's this rule-breaking style that's won my heart. I have set out on a journey to make an art out of supplying my kitchen. I can only guarantee one thing, there will be no straight lines.

POLYCULTURE

Growing more than one species or variety of vegetable together is called polyculture, contrasting with monoculture where you grow a single species. An organic garden that grows more than one type of vegetable is a type of polyculture, but true polyculture is to grow a variety of plants together that will benefit from being in an ecological community. Perhaps the best-known version of this idea is the 'Three Sisters', the traditional Native American way of growing beans, corn and courgettes or pumpkins together. The beans grow up the corn and courgettes scramble around the base. The beans lend nitrogen to the hungry corn, the corn acts as stakes for the beans to climb up and the courgettes act as a living mulch, conserving water and keeping weeds down. Together, the three make a community. Polyculture is a new name for a very ancient way of farming that aims to mimic natural ecosystems by following nature's pattern.

More complex polycultures can use up to nine different species. Here, radishes, lettuces, cabbages, pot marigolds and parsnips are all sown at the same time, each variety being broadcast in drifts across your patch of land. Radishes emerge first, shading the ground and trapping moisture to benefit the other vegetables. As you start to harvest your radishes more vegetables begin to germinate. Regular picking allows each plant to establish its space within the system. Deep-rooted vegetables, such as parsnips, exploit the lower soil and shallow-rooted ones, such as lettuces, exploit the upper soil, which should mean less competition for resources. You do have to thin your crops constantly, but experiments show that given two equal-sized pieces of land you can plant more per area using polyculture methods, with equal or greater plant emergence and although plants do tend to grow more slowly under polyculture, overall yield is usually greater.

There are so many benefits to polyculture. You have reduced pest and disease problems as the crop diversity means it's very hard for pests and diseases to build up to serious numbers. As there is no bare or exposed ground, water is conserved and plants benefit. Also, different species offer different habitats so local biodiversity increases.

You do have to pay more attention to set up and harvest than if you're working in a straight line, but there is little weeding other than regular thinning of plants, and these thinnings are your supper. Polyculture set-up issues are mostly to do with keeping a pleasing vision. A lot of plants need to be raised as small plants in pots ready to go in when a space is available so you don't see great gaps, but if you view this as one way of never running out of food, then perhaps it's not such a drawback.

There are few set rules, and many different combinations, so you have to work out for yourself what will work best for your plot according to your soil, aspect and space. If you decide to adopt the principles of polyculture you are a pioneer of a new form of gardening and you should document every success and failure you have – the more we know, the better the system will work. One of the joys of digital media and mobile technology is that we can share our understanding, so think of polyculture in Wikipedia terms and go out there, and grow, then publish.

I find myself somewhere between poly-culture and edible landscaping, dipping in to both to steal the best bits from each. My garden doesn't have a clear plan to it, except that I try and keep the tall vegetables to the back of the border and shorter vegetables,

and those that need regularly harvesting, to the front. While working to raise the fertility of my soil I have stayed fairly clear of root vegetables, other than the potatoes I'm using to break up the ground and hide the fence. I have direct sown radish, rocket, marigolds, dill and other flowers in drifts, but have interplanted with other vegetables that I've grown in plugs (small individually raised plants), as I've found it easier to create the right layers this way. Every day is a new experiment as I learn what varieties and combinations work for me and my garden.

You do need to know and understand your own local conditions to grow a healthy mix of edible and ornamental plants. The only rules are that you need good soil, light and water if you want good vegetables. I do understand that for many people growing in straight lines is a simple, convenient way of planting and harvesting, but I have found that growing in a careful muddle is surprisingly simple once you've got your head around the principles. All gardening is endlessly interesting, discovering what grows best where and with what, whether its conventional straight lines or not, but when you muddle up flowers, fruit and vegetables rather than separating them, you end up looking out for all parts of your garden at the same time. You notice more about what's going on, your vegetable garden is never out of sight and out of mind, but ever present. Instead of having to go to just one part of my garden to pick my supper I now have to wander through my garden, thinning salads for my supper, watching new vegetables grow and emerge, keeping my fingers crossed for the tomatoes and eagerly awaiting the first potatoes. It seems so obvious, but my first

urban vegetable garden was at the bottom of my narrow terrace garden and I would rush back from work and either run past the top half of the garden, not even noticing it, or I wouldn't get to the bottom at all. No other form of gardening has brought me closer to the space and to understanding my role within it – which turns out to be surprisingly little, as I do more eating than battling with pests.

LOCAL LOVE

I cannot teach you about your local knowledge, or about local love and loyalty, except to say that in order to know your place, and where you belong, you need to understand that you are part of an ecosystem far bigger than your needs, and that you are responsible for its health and must be a good caretaker.

When you grow your own vegetables, herbs and cut flowers you start to actively contribute to your local economy. It's not just about spending less money, though you will definitely spend less on groceries (and gym memberships), but about becoming more aware. When you work your soil and produce your own food you begin to understand all the limitations that come with natural abundance, you come to realize that you cannot exhaust the soil year on year (or exhaust yourself). You start to want to buy things differently, particularly handmade, crafted, local or loved products that are made by people rather than corporations. When you develop your own skills and self-mastery you start to recognize and admire the skills of others. You will increasingly notice what's going on locally and you'll start to want to buy things differently.

You will always have to buy things in order to grow your own, whether it's the initial set up cost of bringing in good compost, repairing old tools or buying new plants and seeds, but by growing your own you will start to recover a proportion of economic responsibility that is not about the boom and bust of cheap commodities sold at the highest prices and made at the lowest (and always at a cost to the earth).

You may also quickly become part of a local network. You'll find people who will give you animal manure, or swap plants, and people to help you water when you're away. You may join community gardens and gardening groups, and generally begin to pay more attention to your community.

Looking after your local surroundings is a pleasing responsibility and brings all sorts of rewards with it. Some of these are obvious – you eat them – but others will only become apparent when you stand back a little.

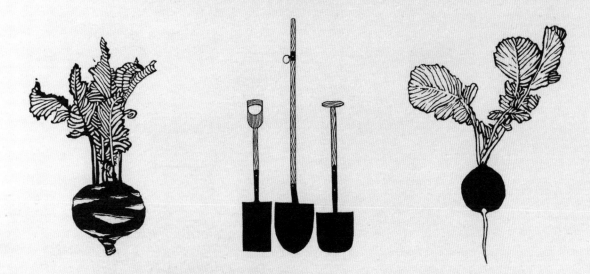

THINGS TO KNOW

In order to reap the rewards of a bountiful garden you need to know some things, such as what type of soil you have and how to make your plants happy. By arming yourself with the basics you can start to plot and plan meals from your back garden and beyond.

The New Order

I think this has been a long time coming.

For a while I have kept my subversive gardening thoughts to myself. So I may have put the odd patch of flowers at the end of the vegetable bed (a little whimsy), or left the rocket recklessly to flower (a moment of weakness), or grown clover under the cucumbers – but it could all be seen as just an experiment.

It's only possible to keep quiet for so long, or in my case until I started to notice others coming out of the wilderness. I'd read about their work on the net, or they'd noticed the way I'd done something, and suddenly we were all admitting our own mildly eccentric growing patterns to each other. At the beginning of the year someone came into my garden and said, 'Oh I like growing weeds too'. This was one of the foremost organic gardeners in the country, a woman with not a lazy bone in her green fingers, recognizing that the sterility of traditional growing methods might not work for everyone.

When I was recently brambling (botanical rambling) over the Internet, looking for some fellow polyculture growers, I came across the site Punk Rock Permaculture e-zine. I knew then that things are changing, and rather rapidly. Punk Rock Permaculture is an online magazine dedicated to the cooler side of permaculture. Its tag line is 'a place to make places better'. Entries have included simple DIY medicinal herb gardens, how to rip up your lawn to grow vegetables, and something called a 'permaculture geek rap', a hip hop rap about how to make the world a healthier place. The point is not so much about the site, though I'd recommend a visit, but that a young man in the US is writing about growing vegetables using a language that absolutely no-one would have predicted five years ago – slightly anarchic, a little punkish, it reads more like an album review than a site on environmentalism. Growing vegetables is one part of the way he defines himself, along with

Right: My muddle of flowers and vegetables provides plenty of salads by June. 'Australian Yellow Leaf' lettuce contrasts with the reds of 'Bresson Rouge' lettuce. Garlic is dotted between the young dwarf beans, dark leaves of Tuscan black kale provide contrast at the back.
Overleaf: For the vase: cool blues of Eryngiums and opium poppy seed heads in late August.

bike riding, eco-building, punk folk and cooking veggies. He's not alone and is part of a growing body of urban growers who are young, hip and cool.

These younger voices have created a breathing space that allows us to step back and look at how we go about growing and talking about food. It's obvious that there is a way that's not all straight lines and wide spacing, that's not necessarily about owning a certain sort of land or being a certain sort of grower. By letting go of some of the formalities of traditional growing, we can begin to express food growing in slightly more romantic, perhaps some would say frivolous, terms.

Call it floral food, edible landscaping, ornamental vegetable gardening, call it what you like, but if you want to grow courgettes in your borders, plant cabbages on roundabouts, grow your lettuce amongst the flowers, if you do the best part of your gardening in bare feet, if your garden isn't behind your house, then welcome to another way.

Here is how I see it. Why plant any old plant when it could be edible, or useful? Why not replace all those shrubs and small trees in your garden that give little more than a burst of seasonal interest with a fruit tree, redcurrants and blueberries? I want a beautifully productive garden that weaves together flowers, fruit and vegetables in a way that mimics natural systems so that nature and I can get along peacefully together. No battles with pests, no need to exhaust the soil, just enough vegetables for my table and enough of everything else to make it balanced. The tallest order is that it has to be an aesthetically pleasing mixture that in time will evolve to be more productive as I grow with it.

HOW TO MIX TREES, EDIBLES AND FLOWERS

From the start I have to admit that there is no plan – no regime, no particular order or rules to abide by, just recommendations. Your own experience teaches you more than anything else, so you will need to take a big breath and leap forward.

First you need to assess what is already in your garden, what it's worth to you, how productive it is, and what you can change. I have a magnolia tree at the bottom of my garden that does not give me a single thing to eat, but every spring it makes my heart sing as it bursts into flower well before the rest of the garden has woken up. A quince would flower in a similar way, an apple tree would give me lovely flowers as well as a vast amount of fruit, even a hazel would be more productive. But I love that magnolia, it was one of the reasons I bought the house. It stays.

On the other hand Leyland cypress, willow, poplar, ash, large eucalyptus are all huge trees that can rob a garden of productivity. Leyland cypress in particular makes the soil below dry and barren. If you have a large, ugly conifer or a tree that leaves your garden in shade, think about taking it out. You don't have to remove all existing trees, you can work around lots of them, but if you want fruit trees and vegetables a garden does need to get good light and have soil that is not already filled up with other roots.

If you are going to add fruit trees – and every garden should have at least one – think carefully where to put them. Don't try to move a tree once you have established it. If you're not sure of its

A happy mix: calendula and kale are brilliant contrasts and the flowers bring in plenty of beneficial insects to keep pests off the kale.

final destination move it around to a few different locations in the pot that you bought it in, and think about it for a few days before planting it.

Fruit bushes, such as currants and raspberries, need similar thought. Some soft fruit will grow under the canopy of an existing tree, but it will grow tall and thin as it searches for light. If you are establishing young fruit trees and fruit bushes at the same time you also need to think about them competing for space to get their roots established.

PLANTING IN DRIFTS

The flower and vegetable layer of your garden is the easiest to sort out. Other than perennial vegetables, various brassicas and perennial flowers, such as rose bushes, most of the things you'll plant for an edible landscape will live out their life in a year or less. So there's always next year to get it right, you can experiment and learn from the lessons. Play around with very short-lived vegetables, such as radish or lettuce, if they didn't work out in one place try them somewhere else with the next batch, by the end of one season you'll have a good idea of the best spots.

The one thing you can't ignore is spacing. All vegetables and flowers have an optimal spacing distance from their neighbours to allow them to grow big, fast. The key is to grow things in drifts. You can take a bare patch of land and sow several different vegetables across it, using the same space for one batch after another, thinning out as they grow. But it is far simpler to grow plants of similar sizes and shapes together in a graceful drift.

A drift is a group of five or more plants of the same variety planted together, generally in a teardrop shape that is thicker in the middle and further apart on the outsides. This planting pattern is not new. The highly influential Arts and Craft movement designer Getrude Jekyll was known for her painterly style of planting, using drifts of colour in her gardens. And drifts are what nature does best. Go for a walk in the woods or rubberneck on a train journey and you'll see wild plants in great drifts, from rosebay willow herb along railway lines to great stands of bluebells in woods. They weave in and out, getting thicker and thinner, but staying together. You occasionally find a few plants dotted around singly, but more often than not they sit around in gangs.

Using drifts of vegetables in an edible garden means creating a band of, say, lettuce around a courgette, or a drift

of radishes along the edge of large, slower growing vegetables. You can give the majority the spacing they require, making a few compromises around the margins. The microecology of your garden can vary quite considerably, even in a comparatively small space, so any part of your garden can go from relatively damp and shady to hot and sunny in a matter of a few dozen centimetres, rather than metres. Drifts allow you to work with your soil and its conditions, placing sun-lovers in the sun and so on. Much like block plantings (rather than rows), drifts have an advantage over some pests. A straight line of

A weave of red lettuces nestle under a young courgette. The lettuce will be picked before the courgette grows to its full size.

Opposite: Sunshine and shelter: 'Brown Turkey' fig and 'Brandt' grape take advantage of my hot patio.
Below right: Vertical gardening: runner beans 'White Emergo' are tall plants so make sure you put them where you can reach to pick them.

anything a slug likes is fairly easy to ruin, it can just munch its way along it, but a block or drift benefits from safety in numbers. In general, the central plants are held safe, even if the edges are sacrificed.

Look for suitable matches for drift planting. Plant taller-growing vegetables with other flowers or vegetables that will benefit (or won't mind the shade), or exploit different habits by planting deep-rooting carrots with shallow-rooting annual flowers (or *vice versa*). Sweetcorn is relatively thin and tall and the space around its feet is wasted if nothing is planted there. Courgettes, pumpkins and lower growing vegetables can all be used as living mulch to keep the soil moist (which is how corn likes it) and to make the most of available space.

Whatever your style of gardening, one of the most challenging aspects to any method of food growing is getting a continuous and varied supply of food. It is quite easy to get a glut of French beans, or have 40 or so lettuces all ready for the table at the same time. The trick is to have just enough for each night, and to know that there will be more tomorrow.

MAKING THE MOST OF YOUR SPACE

In order to fit in as much as possible, which is both pretty and useful, you need to think cleverly about your space. It may just look like a box, but you can think and grow outside of that. Within every garden there are different microclimates, meaning that the temperature, wind, even moisture will change across the space. You can't grow kiwi or peaches in the middle of most gardens, but if you have a sheltered, sunny (south or southwest facing) wall or fence it's a perfect microclimate for tender fruit. Brick walls are particularly good as bricks absorb heat through the day and release it slowly overnight, keeping the plant that bit warmer.

Most gardens will have spaces you can exploit to your advantage, possibly sunny south-facing corners or sheltered spots against the house for tender fruit, or for

coldframes. My garden slopes away from the house and the patio wall is a perfect suntrap. It faces southwest and the patio stands about 1m (40in) above the garden. I grow cucumbers and tomatoes that like the heat against the retaining wall, and come winter I place old windowpanes against the wall to create a simple coldframe for winter greens. Whatever winter sun appears, this wall will catch it so the glass panes will make the most of any possible solar gain.

Along the deliciously hot and sheltered back walls of my patio, I'm growing a vine and fig, both perfectly suited to baking in the midday sun. They're underplanted with lavenders, thyme and rosemary, all happy in the heat and content with the dry conditions typical beside walls. The soil is thin and not terribly rich, but if I was to add a lot of organic matter to retain moisture and feed the soil I could grow tomatoes, perhaps even aubergines, that would also enjoy this sheltered hot spot.

Before planting any fruit trees you must think about when and where the frost comes into your garden. Frost pockets are areas that never thaw out on the coldest days. They are patches of cold air, usually caused by hollows or dips or at the bottom of a slope. Placing an apple tree in a frost pocket probably makes no difference to the tree in late winter, but if that pocket is still there in spring when the tree comes into flower, flowers may be unable to form or may be frosted off.

Wind can be a serious enemy, no plant can thrive if it is constantly beaten by drying harsh winds. Unfortunately in urban areas this problem is compounded by tall buildings. Wind is driven between them and channelled into streams of air that often can't escape, so whips round and round, pushed up over solid buildings only to drop down again into the next empty space. The best windbreaks are ones that allow the wind through, but slow it down, rather than impervious barriers. Living windbreaks, such as deciduous trees or hedges, are good, evergreen trees are more problematic as their foliage can act like a sail, making them vulnerable in very windy conditions. Living windbreaks do, however, compete with other plants for light, nutrients and water.

Robust and fast-growing plants can help reduce wind, Jerusalem artichokes have long been popular around the edges of vegetable gardens for this reason, sunflowers and sweetcorn can help a bit, though they

Baby gherkins start their journey upwards in an old bath. Meanwhile the space below is put to good use with lettuce and a young tomato.

will probably need staking. You can erect temporary windbreaks, such as the sort you might use on a beach, to protect young crops. Hessian sacking and beach windbreaks can create a protective microclimate.

EXPECTATION OF HARVEST

It is incredibly hard to be self-sufficient in vegetables without dedicating a lot of your time to growing, for that you really have to treat your plot almost like a job. But I get a meal a day through the summer with what I consider little effort. There are times when the garden expects a lot from me, and times when it is undemanding. As I am happiest in my garden, dedicating time to it is an easy and natural thing to do.

We all (even me) need to have reasonable expectations about what can be achieved, both in terms of the space and the time we have available. Be very pleased if you can eat a salad every day you wish. If you can create a whole meal for those that you love from your garden, that is a grand achievement and nothing to be mocked at in your first year. If your space is limited to a balcony, then producing your own fresh and dried herbal tea is inspiring enough, and will make a difference to your bank balance and your footprint.

Even in the most productive gardens it's hard to avoid hungry gaps; late spring is notoriously difficult when winter greens, kales and cabbages are ending and early summer salads aren't yet ready. Here I rely, in part, on foraging in my local parks and wilder areas of the city to provide me with nettle soup and wild salads until my garden gets going.

FORAGING

There is a time in any garden when you have to harvest elsewhere, because of the time of year, because you forgot to sow something, you've run out of greens or just because the bounty elsewhere is too good to miss. Even within city limits you can pick masses of lovely food for free.

Foraging for anything other than blackberries is not about quantity, wild foods offer small amounts to be gathered here and there. It takes time, it's about knowing your place – where the best mushrooms appear or where the largest stand of wild strawberries grow. It is deeply satisfying and links us indelibly to the land. Reclaiming parks and wild areas as part of our culinary landscape is important – if you care to eat something, then you care to protect that bit of land and your right to go harvesting. We might even be able to control some rampant plants, such as Japanese knotweed and Himalayan balsam, if more people knew how to eat them.

My earliest memory of wild food is my mother picking young hawthorn leaves with unbelievable glee that spring had arrived. She took me around the garden and pointed out what you could and couldn't eat, which flowers were full of nectar, which were the sweetest grasses to chew. I took these memories and half-remembered lessons with me when I moved to the city, and each spring I wander with the dog and nibble hawthorn leaves with just as much glee.

SOME RULES OF FORAGING

● Don't forage in Scientific Interest and National Nature Reserves without the express permission of Natural England.

● On private land you need the permission of the landowner before you can dig or uproot any plant. It is illegal to collect plants or fungi for commercial purposes without the landowner's permission. However, you can pick (not dig) them up for your own use.

● Certain plants, such as the mint pennyroyal, are protected by law and it is illegal to collect them without a license.

● Be a sustainable forager and only take what you need. Harvest respectfully, seeds and flowers are the plant's future.

Not just for eating: collecting comfrey for plant food.

Linden flowers for tea from the small-leaved lime tree.

● Understand your poisonous plants. Some plants look edible, but are deadly. Go foraging with someone who knows the difference until you are entirely sure what's what.

● Take a good reference book with you.

● Know which stage of the plant you should eat. Understand there are some herbs and wild plants that are fine to eat except if you're pregnant or breast-feeding.

● Take a good knife, secateurs, gloves and plenty of bags (paper if you're picking mushrooms as they sweat in plastic).

● Tackle roots cautiously and triple-check identification. If you gather roots, you kill the plant or part of it, so only collect them where there are plenty of plants and only take what you need. Wild horseradish is very strong, so you need less than you'd expect.

● Pick mushrooms extremely cautiously. I am only really happy with a few obvious ones. The rest I leave alone unless I'm with an expert.

● Consider pesticides, herbicides, pollutions and dog pee. Think about all that could, might and will have drifted onto your plants and pick wisely.

In spring young leaves are tender and soft, and your garden is least productive. Pick young nettle leaves, sticky cleavers, ground elder, garlic mustard, dead nettles, and delicious wild garlic or rampions that are only around in spring. I forage my way out of the hungry gap with nettle soups, wild green stir-fries and spring salads. Many balms, dead nettles and red nettles can be eaten into early summer, with pignut and sheep's sorrel. Late summer and autumn are the seasons of plenty, beginning with wild raspberries, then Mahonia berries and Darwin's berry *Berberis darwinii*, then the many blackberries, bilberries, sea-buckthorn, guelder rose, elders, sloes, damsons, hawthorn and juniper berries that I bottle, dry and jam for winter supplies.

THE NO-DIRT SOLUTION: GROWING IN POTS

It's one thing to play around with how to grow in the ground, but what if you don't own a patch to plant into? I have always found growing food in pots easier than in the soil as conditions are controllable, and with good compost, regular watering and good light you can get very good results. One of the joys of growing in pots is that you can move them around. This not only gives them the best possible chance as the season progresses, but you can place plenty of flowers and nectar-rich plants between your vegetables to create an ecology that will attract beneficial insects and pollinators to your pots, or you can grow the two together in large pots.

I also like to try and create a soil ecology within the pots. I often add excess composting worms from the worm bin to larger pots, though the climate within a pot can get rather hot for this sort of worm so you tend to find them congregating at the base of the pot if it all gets a bit much. They need a regular source of organic matter to feed on so

don't overtidy the pot, as dead and dying leaves act as a good source of food. Every time I empty a pot, I am surprised by how many worms I find. They do sterling work, as the soil in pots can get very compacted and soil without enough air is very detrimental to plants. These worms and all the other fauna that follow them, create drainage channels that allow air and water to move more freely through the pot. In turn, this promotes deep rooting plants, which are better able to withstand drought than those rooting near the surface.

WHAT CONTAINERS CAN YOU GROW IN?

There is no ideal container, it just needs to provide enough room for a decent root run; if it is too shallow or too small the plant will quickly dry out. The cheapest pot is a growbag – a plastic bag filled with potting compost, often formulated for growing vegetables and providing a set amount of food. They tend to be long and shallow and I think a better solution is just to buy a bag of top-quality compost for containers and cut the top off (or lie the bag on its side and cut planting holes in the plastic), make some sort of drainage hole and plant away. Vegetables like cucumber and tomatoes need support – either trellis, manufactured

Above: Sow a line of snapping peas thickly for tender young shoots.
Opposite: An autumn decorative edible display combines red lettuce, kale and violas.

DECORATIVE, EDIBLE VEGETABLES FOR POTS

Many colourful recipes work just as well in pots as they do in the ground.

French marigold and dwarf tomatoes.

Marigolds and Swiss chard.

Golden feverfew and red lettuce, such as 'Lollo Rosso'.

Curly parsley and blue and white splashed violas, such as *Viola* 'Rebecca' or 'Elaine Quinn'.

Red chard and purple violets (look out for the trailing Friolina violas) or purple nemesias or trailing lobelia (though the latter two aren't edible).

New Zealand spinach with golden oregano.

Chilli pepper, golden oregano and red mustard, such as 'Red Frills'.

Variegated land cress, left to go to flower where the lovely white and green splashed leaves are crowned with yellow flowers, and yellow Friolina violets.

Basil and strawberries.

Curly parsley and strawberries.

Wild strawberries and heartsease violas.

Mustard greens ('Red Frills', 'Gold Streak', 'Art Green') in various combinations.

Rainbow chard and nasturtiums.

Kales, such as 'Cavolo Nero' and 'Red Russian' with winter pansies in deep reds and purples.

supports or homemade. You may prefer to plant these in pots deep enough to insert canes or pea sticks. Top-quality compost usually has about six week's worth of food, after that you will have to feed every two weeks or so with liquid feed.

COMPOST

Spend your money on the compost, not the pot. Good container compost needs to have enough food to sustain the plant until harvest, so steer clear of compost that is sold for cuttings or seed-raising, as these have few nutrients because the plants are not expected to stay long in the compost.

Garden soil is not ideal for containers, it's too heavy and tends to get waterlogged with heavy watering, instead steer towards peat-free composts designed for container or vegetable growing. These are usually made

from recycled materials, anything from chicken feathers to shredded palettes and you get what you pay for so buy the best you can afford. Soil-based composts have their place, as they usually hold more nutrients and moisture than recycled composts, but they drain less well and are certainly too heavy to use on balconies or roof gardens. There's also growing concern that the topsoil in the compost is not a renewable resource, and carting soil from one part of the country to another is not sustainable. Multipurpose potting compost can be very hit or miss. It tends to be nutrient-poor and usually needs extra sand, grit or leafmould added for drainage.

The most sustainable compost is one you make yourself, but you need to produce a lot of garden compost to do this. If you don't have enough space to make large volumes,

MINIMUM POT DEPTHS

Carrots 20cm (8in) unless you choose to grow stubby, round types.

Parsnips 45cm (18in).

Coriander 15cm (6in).

Courgettes and squash 45cm (18in).

Cucumbers 45cm (18in).

Cut-and-come-again salad such as oriental greens 10cm (4in).

Horseradish 45cm (18in).

Leaf radish 10cm (4in).

Lettuce 15cm (6in).

Mints 15cm (6in) and at least 30cm (12in) wide.

Parsley 20cm (8in).

Pea shoots 15cm (6in).

Perilla 15cm (6in).

Potatoes 45cm (18in).

Spring onion/Japanese bunching onions 15cm (6in).

Strawberries 10cm (4in).

Thyme 10cm (4in).

Tomatoes 45cm (18in), (you can get away with smaller, but in hot weather you will have to water at least twice a day).

just adding a layer of homemade compost to the top of a pot and digging it in a bit before you sow a new crop will do wonders for the plant.

Homemade composts for containers need to be made up of roughly equal parts garden loam, well-rotted compost, mushroom compost, worm compost or a mixture of the three with a little coarse sand, grit or leafmould to lighten the load and add drainage. You make leafmould by composting autumn leaves in bin bags pierced with holes, and leaving them somewhere out of the way for a year.

CONSERVING WATER IN CONTAINERS

Careful watering is vital for all container-grown plants, even in damp weather as you can't rely on rain to give the pots a thorough soak. Most containers need watering every day through summer and the smaller the pot the more often you'll have to water. Expect to water twice a day in hot, sunny weather, preferably first thing in the morning or in early evening. If you water midday most will evaporate and you'll need to use twice the amount or more.

Drainage is very important, you need to strike a balance between holding the right amount of moisture in a pot and not letting it hang around as plant roots will die from lack of oxygen if they sit in water. Where possible, raise your containers on bricks, blocks of wood or slates so that they sit off the ground to help drainage. Keep containers out of strong wind so plants don't dry out too fast.

Lining pots with a thick layer of newspaper helps hold moisture and the paper will slowly rot. Paper will also insulate metal containers from extreme temperatures. Terracotta pots can be lined with strips of strong plastic, such as pieces of compost bags, to stop them from drying out. You should also mulch the top of large pots with a 5cm (2in) thick layer of stones, gravel, straw or bark to conserve water.

*Old school kitsch: ornamental cabbage
leaves can be used as colourful
garnishes for soups and salads.*

Growing Healthy Plants

There is huge satisfaction in a beautiful, productive garden.

The secret is to grow soil rather than vegetables. If you can get the soil right, the rest will follow almost effortlessly. Healthy, rich soil produces strong plants that can (within reason) withstand pest and disease problems, grow nutritionally complex vegetables and fruit, and support a vast ecology of micro fauna, bacteria and fungi.

Intensive agriculture and increasing urbanization has left our soil in a dire state. Unsustainable practices, such as over-use of fertilizers, shorter fallow periods (the time when the land is not being used to grow a crop), climate change or just burying good soil under concrete have affected the world's resource of topsoil. It is estimated that we have lost a third of farmland due to soil degradation. Couple that figure with a growing population and the picture's rather alarming. Having a beautiful, productive garden is not just personally satisfying, it is crucial for our future. Healthy soil means healthy people, healthy communities and essentially a healthy planet.

But having a productive garden mustn't and shouldn't be just about the greater good, but about the small, honest good that comes from growing your own in a pleasing way. A garden of flowers and fruit and plenty of vegetables is a tangible, beautiful thing.

SOIL FERTILITY

We are our soil, or at least our vegetables are. If you want high-quality, beautiful vegetables then you need rich, fertile soil, preferably that you've made yourself.

A garden that has been mostly lawn, flowers and shrubs will probably have soil that is fairly low in organic matter. One of the first tasks of edible landscaping is to work in as much bulky organic matter as possible. In order to work it into the soil it must be well rotted – animal manure, bird feathers, sheep wool, shredded bark, wood, straw, cardboard, thick newspaper or compost are all ideal. Organic matter plays a pivotal role in soil health because where there is organic matter there will be earthworms,

Good homemade compost is worth its weight in gold.

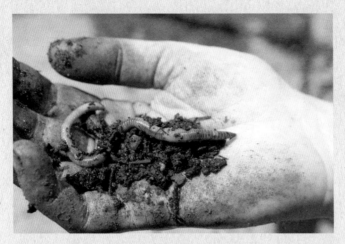

and where there are worms all is right with the world.

Earthworms eat organic matter and poo it out as humus. This is plant food, holding essential nutrients in just the right form for your vegetables and flowers to grow strong. Worms also play an important role in creating the right soil structure. As they burrow about looking for food, they create channels for the air and water that healthy roots need. When worms appear so too do other important soil fauna, microbes and bacteria and when you find worms in your soil you know you have a healthy ecosystem. Learn to love them, don't leave them to dehydrate on the soil surface, try not to chop them in half (they don't grow back), count them (ten worms per spadeful of soil and you're on your way to truly great vegetables) and feed them. There is no such thing as too many worms, even when they die they act as a rich source of nutrients.

Some of the best, certainly the cheapest, soil food is homemade compost. Every garden should have a compost bin of one design or another – you get back what you put in to a garden, and you'll need to keep adding organic matter to the soil every year. Once you've got a compost system up

and running you can become self-sufficient in good organic matter quite quickly, but at the beginning you'll have to look at bringing it in from elsewhere. Many councils offer cheap green waste compost. This is the stuff you put out in green bags that is turned into a very fine grade compost. It's a good starting point. There are also plenty of good shop-bought composts, but for the planet's sake choose a peat-free one. Peat is not sustainable and peat bogs are an important and endangered habitat.

DIGGING THE GOODNESS IN

How you incorporate your organic matter depends a little on how your garden looks. If you are starting with a blank canvas then you can dig it in, but if your garden is planted up you can only add to the soil surface, which is how most organic matter is added in nature – think of leaf litter in a wood. Most biological activity (moving, wiggling creatures, bacteria and fungi) occurs in the top five per cent of the soil, so this is where most of the organic matter needs to be concentrated. Deep-rooted vegetables draw their food from lower down so it is useful to incorporate some organic matter into the bottom of a planting hole.

If you're starting from scratch with bare soil, particularly if it is either very sandy or heavy clay, you'll need to add a large amount of manure or organic matter. Heavy clay needs to be opened up to allow aeration,

drainage and root penetration, so you'll need to mix the organic matter thoroughly through the soil. Only add properly rotted down compost, otherwise you will create unhealthy pockets of anaerobic matter that produce methane through the soil.

If you have very chalky or sandy soil it will be very porous so nutrients will move quickly through it. Simply add the organic material to the soil surface and allow nature to take it deeper into the soil. As it gets incorporated it acts like a sponge, increasing the soil's ability to hold water and hang on to nutrients.

My garden is fairly cluttered with perennials and shrubs so it's not possible to dig in my compost. Instead I add it in autumn to the soil surface (letting my worms dig it in) and incorporate good amounts

into each planting hole as I establish new vegetables. I don't over tidy in the autumn, but allow most of the dead leaves to remain and rot down naturally.

GUIDE TO MAKING YOUR OWN COMPOST

Making good compost is a bit like making a cake. The ingredients need to be in the right proportions. You need roughly two-thirds carbon to one-third nitrogen, which translates as a lot more brown stuff than green. The brown stuff (carbon) comes from fibrous material, such as twigs, woody stems, straw and cardboard, so stop sending your recycling to the kerb and add it to the compost instead. Green stuff is fresh

A BALANCED MEAL

All plants need certain nutrients to grow. Organic fertilizers, such as seaweed sludge, homemade compost and animal manure, have varying degrees of nutrients, but are rich in humus. Manufactured fertilizers on the other hand are concentrated, have little humus and are valued for their mineral content. Most plant foods are made up of Nitrogen, Phosphorus and Potassium (NPK). These are essential elements needed for plant growth. Nitrogen promotes leafy green growth, without which leaves turn yellow. Phosphorus is needed for flower and fruit formation, too little gives you purplish leaves and stems. Potassium is needed for cell division in the roots and affects the plants ability to withstand drought and cold. If there is too little the plant often looks mottled or has curled leaves. Homemade compost is your best and cheapest cure for poor soils, but container-grown plants and hungry, heavy croppers, such as tomatoes, will need liquid feeds every two weeks throughout the growing season.

leaves, grass clippings, flowers, weeds and soft stems.

Try to build your compost up in layers, no more than 15cm (6in) deep. The more air (and moisture) you give your compost the more efficiently the bacteria will work as oxygen is vital to the aerobic bacteria that break down compost. The faster they work, the hotter your compost gets and more weeds, seeds, pathogens and plant diseases get thoroughly broken down.

If you are using a plastic Dalek (the council black compost bin) I recommend drilling holes around the base to let more air in, otherwise the bin can quickly produce anaerobic conditions and slimy compost. Wooden, square bins made from recycled palettes are good, as you can make more than one if you have space so you can turn one bin into the next. The simplest square bin is just a cage of wire mesh around four stakes, and you can even make a bin out of an old chest freezer (called a hot box). There are endless designs and how-to's on the Internet.

THINGS TO COMPOST
Vegetable waste, tea bags, coffee grounds, dog hair, human hair and toilet roll centres will all add to the mix, but steer clear of dairy, meat or fish waste. Don't add any dog, cat or non-vegetarian animal poo. Cardboard, pizza boxes, shredded paper, scrunched up newspaper and cereal boxes can all go in, but stay clear of highly-coloured, glossy paper as it's full of chemicals. Branches and roots that are thicker than your thumb need to be bashed and chopped up otherwise they take an age to compost.

Perennial weeds such as dock, bindweed, ground elder and horsetails need to be rotted down separately in a bucket of water with a lid. When you can no longer make

Left: By the end of the summer your compost bin should be bursting. Turn it to find the good stuff and spread as autumn mulch.

has long, thick taproots that grow deep into the ground and take up nutrients, chiefly potassium (which enhances the flavour and colour of fruit and vegetables and increases drought-tolerance), some calcium, iron and a little phosphorus (essential for flower and fruit formation). The plant stores these nutrients in its leaves so you can harvest them, rot them down in a bucket and then feed them back to your vegetables – plant eats plant. The best comfrey grows where there is a high level of nitrogen, which it also accumulates in its leaves, so it's a good plan to grow it next to an open compost bin where nitrogen leaches out regularly. The best variety is Russian comfrey called 'Bocking 14'. It's sold in spring as root cuttings, but is generally only available from organic seed catalogues.

Comfrey is not only a good plant feed, but a traditional country remedy to heal cuts, bruises and sprains. It can also help to heal plants, if you wrap a comfrey leaf around a plant wound it will speed up healing because comfrey contains allantoin – a cell proliferant that boosts healing.

out any of the weeds pour the liquid mess back on the compost. That way you get all the nutrients back without any pesky weed roots.

LIQUID LOVE

Next to making compost, I urge everyone to grow their own comfrey plant – or patch if you have room. Comfrey is a large plant with lovely purple flowers that are often covered in bees, but its what's happening below ground that makes comfrey so important. It

HOW TO MAKE COMFREY TEA

Don't cut comfrey as it gets established in its first year, but from the second year on you can cut it to the ground at least three times a year. Comfrey feed is particularly good for fruiting crops, such as tomatoes, cucumbers and aubergines.

Rot down the leaves and stems in a bucket of water, with a lid, stuffing in as many leaves as possible, chopping them up to speed up decomposition. The brew is ready when you can't get near it as it stinks (hence the lid). Then water it onto plants, undiluted. You can make a concentrated form by rotting

WHEN TO USE LIQUID FEEDS

OUTDOOR TOMATOES: When the first flowers begin to set fruit. However, if the plant is going yellow, verging on purple, then you should have started earlier. The remedy for this is to feed the plant with a solution of Epsom salts, as it has a lack of magnesium.

COURGETTES: When you first start picking the crop.

CHILLIES: When the fruit begins to swell, but be careful not to overfeed – twice in a season is plenty.

LEEKS: Occasional liquid feed throughout the growing season.

ALL ROOT VEGETABLES, EXCEPT POTATOES: Occasional liquid feed throughout the growing season. Carrots benefit from a worm compost dressing once the roots appear at the surface of the soil.

BRASSICAS: Occasional liquid feed throughout the growing season.

CUCUMBERS: As you start picking the first fruit. They will also benefit from a worm or organic compost dressing around the roots.

down only the leaves under a weight, it takes longer, but doesn't smell as bad.

A similar 'tea' can be made with young nettles in spring. This is rich in nitrogen, but has much lower levels of other nutrients. It's a good pick-me-up for young vegetables, and a combination of nettle and comfrey teas is ideal as the two complement each other well in terms of nutrient balance.

The general rule of thumb is that vegetables grown in healthy soil, full of organic compost, won't need extra feeding, but those that grow in pots or poor soils in their first year will need a little help. This is when liquid feed really comes into its own.

GREEN MANURES

Traditionally, soils were fed with farmyard manure rich in mineral nutrients, which used to be free and plentiful. But these days it's hard to find, difficult to transport and rarely in a state suitable for organic gardeners (who'd want chicken manure from battery hens?). It can be bought in bags from a garden centre and is good stuff, but not cheap. The best substitute is nothing more than a packet of seeds.

Green manure is easy, cheap and an excellent substitute for animal manure. The seed packets are bumper big and for a small garden a single packet, stored properly (cool, dark, moisture-free), will last years. Green manures are super plants. They are sown thick and they're fast growing so they quickly form a canopy across the soil surface. Chosen for their ability to accumulate certain nutrients, they're the equivalent of multivitamins for the soil. Once they are hoed or dug up they break down, releasing

their entire store of nutrients, thus feeding the soil and the crop that follows. They also add fresh organic matter to the soil, like a breakfast bar for worms and other soil organisms who start appearing in great numbers. And when you've got lots of worms you've got soil that can produce bumper veg.

Green manures fall into three camps, nitrogen-fixing manures, such as clovers and field beans, quick-growing leafy types and those with deep fibrous roots. Hungry soils that aren't producing a lot of rich growth get nitrogen-fixing manures, soils that are thin in organic matter and lacking worms get quick growing leafy types, and those that are heavy and difficult to dig get deep-rooted fibrous types (which amazingly actually do the digging for you!).

The most magical are the nitrogen-fixing ones that include field beans, clovers and winter tares (also known as vetches). These plants evolved in nitrogen-poor soils and came to a mutually beneficially agreement with microbes. The microbes invade their roots and live in small nodules (dig up a pea at the end of the season and you'll find hundreds of these white nodules throughout the roots). And here's the miracle, these microbes take nitrogen from the air and 'fix' it so the plant can use it. Nitrogen is not like other plant nutrients, it's not stored in rocks or hanging out in the soil particles, it won't and can't stick around and when there's lots of rain it's dissolved and rushes through the soil. This is known as leaching. These microbes hold onto the nitrogen and store it for the plant. In return the plants feed the microbes.

Growing legumes year on year will improve your soil fertility, as long as you leave the roots (and if possible the stems and leaves) in the plot to rot down. As the plant breaks down it releases all its stored nitrogen for following crops. This is better than adding the whole plant to the compost where nitrogen can be quickly leached away. Once the green manure dies (when you've hoed or dug it in) the nodules start releasing their nitrogen into the soil. When you sow or plant out your next crop they are bedding down in a soil full of nitrogen that is ready for use – nature feeding nature.

Field beans are ideal nitrogen-fixers for compacted soil. Don't let the beans set seed or you lose all the precious nitrogen to the beans and not the soil. Winter tares are brilliant at breaking up tough soil, good at adding matter and they stick around but can be invasive if not ruthlessly hoed. Red and white clovers are my favourites – pretty, delicate and so good at storing nitrogen. Edible peas and beans also release nitrogen. Once you've harvested don't dig them up, but leave the roots (and preferably the leaves and stems chopped up and dug in) behind. This means that any pea or bean that you grow in your garden not only feeds you, but feeds your garden too by enriching the soil with nitrogen.

Quick-growing types are useful between crops. Mustards are up in days and include pretty *Phacelia tanacetifolia* with its fine, lacy foliage and blue flowers loved by bees, green mustards and the buckwheat *Fagropyrum esculentum*, another looker with dainty white flowers and green mustards. These sorts are mainly used to add organic matter to thin soil, but some have the added benefit of accumulating certain key nutrients. Both buckwheat and leafy mustards accumulate phosphates that are essential for flower and fruit formation. Vegetables are greedy and particularly bad at feeding themselves, so

The more you turn your compost the faster it gets made, so get in and get mucky.

you can use buckwheat and mustards to fill the soil up before the vegetables go in. Fast-growing, leafy types of green manures are best sown in early spring for digging in before midsummer. This will add much needed moisture to summer soils. You shouldn't allow them to flower, but as buckwheat and *Phacelia* are so beneficial to insects I see no reason not to leave some to bloom.

Deep fibrous-rooted kinds can be used to break up difficult clay soils, such as grazing rye *Secale cereale*. If *Phacelia* is left to flower it will act in a similar manner, as it establishes deep roots. Grazing rye is incredibly hardy and a good cover for bare winter soil. Sow it in the autumn and dig it back in spring.

The deep roots are good at breaking up difficult soils and the green leaves will store

Light in September – that moment where you can go 'I grew that!'

nitrogen over winter. Bare soil that is left over winter essentially has no nitrogen come spring. A soil wrapped in a blanket of grazing rye, however, is raring to go.

You have to wait three weeks for the rye to break down before you sow (it releases a compound that inhibits germination) and then, *voila*, your soil is starting spring full of life.

ALTERNATIVE USES FOR GREEN MANURES

So far, so traditional – if you have a bare patch of land sow a green manure to improve fertility (and keep the weeds down). But having a bare patch isn't restricted to just the soil in the ground. I grow many of my potatoes and tomatoes in big pots on my patio. By big I mean 100 litre (26.4 gallon) pots, that's an awful lot of compost. I can't produce that much compost and so I have had to buy in peat-free manufactured stuff. I worked out that growing my potatoes cost me £40 a pot in compost – hardly economic sense, even if it was gastronomic heaven. So I set about finding a way to keep the compost in good nick year on year.

Now I grow first early potatoes that I aim to have out by the end of June. I then put all the old foliage from the potatoes at the bottom of the pot, put the compost back in and sow a quick-growing crop like lettuce or radish. In autumn I sow grazing rye that will over winter until spring. Its lush growth looks very sculptural in big pots and it comes through frost and snow well. In spring I dig it back in and start my next crops. If I'm going to use the pots for tomatoes I get one quick-growing crop first, such as mustard or buckwheat. I haven't had to buy in any new compost and I have very healthy pots with the all-important worm activity that is hard to achieve in pots.

I've also taken to using green manures as an understorey crop for certain vegetables. The green manures act as living mulches, conserving water, keeping down weeds and pests and helping to improve the soil structure. By establishing green manure through an existing crop you also get around space issues. In order to successfully establish a green manure for over wintering you need to sow no later than August, which poses a problem for small gardens that are unlikely to have bare ground in late summer.

This way you get both your crop and soil protection through winter.

There are other benefits to this method. If cabbages are undersown with clover, or the ground is left weedy, there is a significant reduction in the number of plant-eating insects, particularly cabbage root fly, cabbage aphid, and, to a lesser effect, both cabbage white butterflies. It appears that the insects use visual cues to know where to land, if everything is green then they can't pin-point exactly what to land on and often land on the wrong thing (the clover). Whereas, if all you plant is cabbages and leave the soil bare then the visual cue is very apparent and all the pests land on the cabbages. I've taken to growing a lot of brassicas this way, sometimes using clover, sometimes whatever's to hand (this year it's buckwheat).

It seems to work best if you establish the green manure crop by mid July, when a lot of the pests get busy. You need your crop to be large enough to compete with the green manure, whilst giving the understorey enough time to establish. I've swamped cabbages in the past because the clover grew too quickly, and if this looks like happening you need to cut the clover back around the crop. The clover re-grows, but at a reduced rate, giving your chosen crop enough room to romp away.

Getting Your Garden Started

The cheapest way to grow your own food is by sowing seed.

A packet of mixed lettuce seed will cost next to nothing, will provide you with more than enough lettuce for this year and still leave you with seed for next. Plug-raised plants bought from garden centres raise the cost of growing your own to nearer supermarket prices. This isn't necessarily a bad way to start off growing vegetables, but seed sowing is simple and very rewarding.

ALL ABOUT SEEDS

If you can understand seeds and how to harness them, then you have at your fingertips the ability to produce healthy, economical meal after meal, whether you're just after sprouts on the kitchen windowsill or pumpkins in the garden.

It is worth buying greenhouse-raised plants if you don't have suitable space to raise seeds and want to grow heat-loving seedlings like cucumbers, chillies, tomatoes and peppers. To get ahead of the season I quite often buy young chilli plants. The best way to get lots of fruit is to raise a chilli plant in a greenhouse and bring it out into the garden for July, so you'll get a better crop if you buy a young, greenhouse-raised plant and grow it on. This also works for tomatoes and sweet peppers.

It can also be worth buying young plants to fill unwelcome gaps. After my tomatoes failed I did a quick buy of some winter kales and Brussels sprouts. The plants cost me just over a pound and I easily made my money back in produce over the following months.

SEED SOWING

The easiest way to sow seeds is into seed trays with good, peat-free seed compost. Shop-bought compost for seeds is sterilized and has just the right structure for seeds to grow in – light, well-drained and not too much food. If you can't get hold of seed

The perfect architecture of a poppy seed head – each chamber is full of next year's promise.

SEED FACTS

• Seeds need several things to germinate. Oxygen, water and temperature are most important. Light is a factor for many seeds. Temperature lets the seed know it's the right time of year, light tells some seeds they are in the right place to germinate, water gets them going. Small seeds such as lettuce need light, but will only germinate when the temperature and water conditions are also right. The smaller the seed, the more likely it is to need light to germinate. Do not bury small seeds.

• Wild plants have complex mechanisms in place to stop germination happening at the wrong time. It's no good for a plant to start life just as we go into winter, so many seeds will only germinate at the right temperature. The warming of wet winter soils in spring activates many seeds but Mediterranean plants often have the opposite trigger, they will not germinate in hot temperatures because this means baking summers are around the corner and seedlings will be fried in the heat. The germination patterns of any particular plant are closely linked to the ecological problems existing in their part of the world.

• You need to help some seeds along to get certain crops going ahead of the season. It's best to start seeds that come from warmer places – tomatoes, peppers, aubergines and other fruit – indoors, where we can offer the right temperatures and moisture and generally monitor things.

• Never add fertilizer to seed compost. Seeds come with their own food source. A seed is an embryo surrounded by a store of food and encased in a tougher outer shell to protect it from extremes of heat, fungal diseases, organisms and predators. A dry seed can't be destroyed by low temperatures.

• Seed compost needs to have an open structure and be water-retentive as seeds need air and water. Either buy special 'seed and cutting compost' or add leafmould, grit or sand to other compost to open it up. Seeds need a continuous supply of moisture to germinate, but if they become waterlogged they die. To keep them moist cover the tray with a propagator lid or clear plastic bag. Once the seedling appears, remove this.

• Seeds need constant temperature, not extremes. If you don't have a propagator, a windowsill in a warm room but out of direct sunlight is best in spring.

• Seeds left in the sun for even a short time are ruined. Always keep seed packets somewhere cool and dry.

compost buy multipurpose peat-free and mix two parts compost to one part sand, grit or leafmould. By sowing in seed trays you can make sure the seeds start life in the very best place, whether it's tomatoes indoors on a warm windowsill or lettuces in a sheltered spot outdoors, away from strong midsummer sun.

A few seeds hate to start life in seed trays, particularly those with long tap roots or fast-growing vegetables like kohl rabi or radishes that find the shallow conditions of seed trays too restrictive. If you don't want to sow direct into the ground you can raise them in modules and plant out healthy, strong plants more able to withstand attacks from slugs and other beasties. It is easier to plan the garden this way, as when one crop comes out another is ready to go straight in, just keep a few spares to replace any that get munched. You can tell when module-raised plants are ready to go out when you just start to see roots emerging from the bottom of the modules.

PRICKING OUT

If you start seed off in a seed tray, at some point you'll have to prick out into modules to allow each seedling its own allocated space. You prick out when the seedlings are large enough to handle. First fill your modules with compost and make a hole in the centre of each little block with your finger, or a pencil, to drop each seedling into. You need to handle the seedling by its seed or baby leaves. These are the first leaves that appear and are often larger than the true leaves, they are there to absorb as much light as possible and to kick start the growing period. Once their job is done they drop off, so if you damage a baby leaf it's far

Right: Sowing lettuce seeds in trays, to be pricked out and potted on for the next gap in the garden.
Overleaf: Pretty as a picture poppies.

WHAT TO SOW WHERE

**ON A WARM WINDOWSILL OR
IN A PROPAGATOR:**

Tomatoes, best at 21° C (70° F).

Lettuce.

Peppers (sweet and chilli), best at
    21° C (70° F).

Aubergines, best at 21° C (70° F).

Squash.

Courgette.

Sweetcorn, in large modules.

Cucumbers.

Perilla.

Broccoli (purple sprouting and nine star).

Basil.

Dill.

Celery.

Cosmos.

Morning glory.

Dahlias.

**IN MODULES OUTSIDE (SOMEWHERE
FROST FREE):**

Parsnips, large modules only.

Lettuce.

Salsola.

Peas.

Beans (French, broad and runner).

Sunflowers, large modules only.

Brassicas (cabbages, kales and cauliflowers).

Swiss chard.

Spinach.

Spring onions.

Beetroot.

Sweet peas.

Pansies.

Violas.

Nasturtiums.

STRAIGHT INTO THE GROUND:

Carrots.

Beetroot.

Radish.

Cut-and-come-again or mix salad bowl
    lettuce.

Hardy annual flowers, such as nigella,
    calendula, honesty and annual poppies.

less drastic than damaging a true leaf. You also should never handle the seedling by the stem. It is so vulnerable at this stage that any sort of bruising can cause trouble later.

The easiest way to prick out is to get a chopstick, pencil or dibber and tease the roots from below, whilst gently tugging at the baby leaves. Once you have lifted up the seedling, continue to support the roots until it is safely in its new home.

Once transplanted you need to water your seedlings in to settle the soil around their roots. Use a watering can with a rose and gently water the seedlings until they are fully drenched. If you don't have a rose then sit the seedlings in a tray of water and allow the compost to become fully soaked from below. Keep the seedlings out of full sun for a while so that they get their roots bedded down.

Seedlings in plugs (just pricked out) are a little drunk on space, but they'll soon stand up straight and get growing.

coldframe, it's also a good place to raise outdoor seedlings.

Once your seedlings are ready for life in the ground they'll have to contend with weeds, pests and diseases. Good healthy soil will always have weeds, it's a sign that the soil is alive, but you don't want weeds smothering young plants, especially when they are establishing.

WEEDS

Once a polyculture system gets established there should be few weeds, as there is little bare ground. The more you mulch with a thick covering of organic matter (homemade compost, bark, straw, newspaper) the less weeding you have to do. Once your seedlings are established in the garden, weed carefully and mulch around them with compost and the best part of the job is done. You'll need a good 8–10cm (3–4in) to smother weed seeds, so mulch as thickly as possible without smothering your young plants.

WHAT TO DO WITH YOUR WEEDS
Annual weeds, such as chickweed, bittercress and herb Robert, can go into your salad, straight onto the compost or into the chicken coop. Perennial weeds should be rotted down in a bucket with water before being sloshed onto the compost. Less invasive ones, such as dandelions, should have the leaves composted, but rot the leaves in a bucket first.

HARDENING OFF

If you have raised seedlings indoors then they need to be hardened off for at least two weeks between the warm, cosseted environment inside and the harsher realities of life in the ground. Harden off in a coldframe, a sheltered outside environment that is protected from the worst of the weather, such as strong winds, rain and frost. You can improvise, a strong cardboard box with a pane of glass is a temporary solution, or bricks stacked in a box shape and covered with glass or fleece. Polystyrene fish boxes are excellent (poke holes through the bottom). In the long term it's worth investing in a sturdy

WATERING

Plants take up all their food via water. Plants grown in the ground are usually more than able to find their own sources of water, particularly if you mulch around establishing plants to help trap water into the soil, but fruit trees will need to be watered regularly during the first couple of years. There is no point planting a tree and ignoring its aftercare, a tree that suffers drought in its second year after planting will be checked in growth for the rest of its life. The bigger the plant the more important it is to make sure it becomes settled in its environment. If you're establishing a lot of fruit trees at once then you may want to bury seeper hoses under the soil surface to help make the job easier, but it's always best to give them a thoroughly good soak every week or so rather than a trickle every day. Healthy plants send their roots deep into the soil, so you need to make sure the water penetrates deep down, not only in the ground, but in pots too.

Every garden should have a water butt to collect rainwater, which is free, unprocessed and often contains lots of naturally occurring nutrients. It also

Pots and containers need a good soak. Leaves, particularly lettuce, are tough and bitter if they don't get enough water.

tends to be relatively pH balanced, whereas tap water can often be very alkaline (hard). This can cause white residue on leaves that reduces their ability to photosynthesize.

PESTS AND DISEASES

One of the major benefits of polyculture is that pest and disease problems are halved because of the layout. A straight line of one single vegetable is asking for trouble, but it's hard for pests or diseases to get a

hold on a wiggly line, interspersed with other vegetables. I can't imagine my garden without every leaf slightly nibbled, to me it's a sign of healthy ecosystem, but a whole plant munched to an inch of its life is something different. The rule of thumb about recognizing the bugs to keep and the bugs to get rid of is that if something runs or moves fast it's probably a good guy, a predator that needs speed to get its supper, so leave it alone. If it's slow to move it's probably a vegetarian and therefore a pest, so get rid of it.

KEEPING THE WOLF FROM THE DOOR

One of the more challenging aspects of food growing is getting a continuous and varied supply of food. It is quite easy to get a glut of French beans or have 40 or so lettuce all coming into fruition at the same time, but it's more tricky to have just enough each evening and to know there will be more tomorrow.

Successional cropping means a continuous supply of food. To make this work you need to know how long a crop takes to mature. Lettuce are ready to crop roughly 12 weeks after sowing and celery will take about 18 weeks before you can cut the first stem (the best way to crop celery is stem by stem rather than whole heads). The easiest way to get successional crops of your favourite, fast-maturing crops, such as lettuce, kohl rabi, radish or young carrots, is to sow the next batch the minute you see the first is up and healthy. If you don't have space in the ground the way around this is to sow in modules, then you never need to have bare soil, as one crop is harvested there is always a plug of something else to fill the gap.

SLUG CONTROL

I squish small slugs between my fingers, and I stamp on the larger ones or slice them in half. I accept it's not pleasant, so if you're not keen on killing them try barrier control.

● Spread a thin, but wide, circle of used coffee grounds around the plant you care about. Slugs can't stand caffeine and the barriers keep working in the rain.

● Sharp grit, broken eggshell and seashells will all make a surface that slugs don't like. Salty seashells work best.

● A barrier of very fine sawdust, bran or oatmeal will dehydrate slugs, but it won't work in the rain when slugs are most active.

● Copper will give slugs mini electric shocks. You can buy commercial copper rings to put round plants and copper tape for pots, or search skips for copper pipe and customise it.

● Cut a small water bottle into rings and use pinking shears to cut jagged top edges. Place the barrier around young plants, the spiky top is like barbed wire to slugs.

With substantial crops, such as apples and currants, you need a longer plan. It may take an apple tree ten years or more to mature to a good size and yield, but you can consider planting shorter term fruiting crops in what will eventually be the shade of the tree. For example, most currant bushes have a life span of around 10–15 years before they need to be renewed, strawberries are good for five years at best.

QUICK FILLERS

Some food plants are really quick to harvest and can be fitted into any unexpected gaps. Radishes and mustards are quick space fillers, within three weeks a radish can supply leaves for stir-frying and steaming, and if you don't manage to harvest all your radishes before they bolt and go to seed you can munch crunchy radish seedpods raw or stir-fried. Windowsill growers (or any impatient gardeners) can get a quick harvest of greens from small seedlings grown to 10cm (4in) tall. Amaranth, Swiss chard, parsley, coriander, lettuce, beetroot and kales can all be used. Cabbages can be made to re-sprout, if you score a cross in the top of the stem about 2cm (1in) deep when you harvest the head, the reshoots can be used as greens. Most cabbage, broccoli and cauliflower stems can be peeled and the soft, pale insides eaten raw or steamed like broccoli. The bits nearest the top usually taste best.

Previous: Cuban oregano or Jamaican thyme is a tender herb that needs to be brought in over winter so is best grown in a pot.

Right: Homemade greenhouse: the stained glass makes perfect dappled light for the tomatoes. Come winter it will house tender herbs and plants for protection against winter weather.

PLANT PROTECTION

Our relatively mild winters and good autumns mean we can keep cropping through most of the year. I can find something to eat in my garden all year round. Bottling and pickling keeps the taste of summer fruits, but for salads all you need is some sort of shelter. Cloches, coldframes and tunnels are all useful to keep the worst of the winter weather off the soil, and means you can sow and harvest winter hardy salads and stir-fry greens. Commercial cloches are a good investment, either dome shaped or mini tunnels with rigid metal frames, covered with fleece that traps heat, but allows water through, or with clear plastic. You can easily make your own using hoops made from plumbing pipe anchored into the soil with stakes as a frame, and covered with bubble wrap, plastic or fleece. If you use plastic remember you'll have to water more often and ventilate on warm days, as conditions can get very humid allowing diseases like the mould botrytis to flourish.

Lamb's lettuce, Oriental greens, rocket, 'Winter Density' lettuce, coriander, some hardy winter spinaches, Oriental radishes and land cress will all grow lush and lovely under winter cover, allowing you to pick until the next spring offers something new. Start sowing winter salads from mid-August and continue sowing batches little and often until the beginning of October.

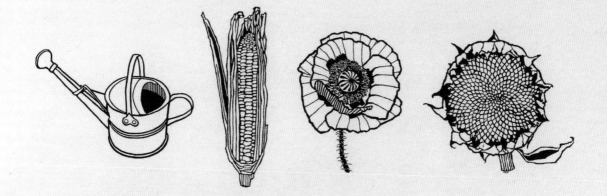

THINGS
TO GROW

There are literally thousands of vegetables and flowers out there. Here's my guide to those that I like because they taste good, provide a plentiful harvest and just look beautiful, from traditional garden staples to some you'd probably never think of eating.

Everything Essential That I Know About Growing Vegetables (and Flowers)

WHAT WOULD NATURE DO?

Where do you start? It can be a bit daunting, looking at your garden and trying to make decisions about what should go where, particularly when you are mixing ornamentals and edibles together. You can't grow everything you'd like to eat, particularly in a small garden. To help you decide, you need to take the time to consider what role a plant will play. I like to consider the process as a conversation between you and the space, asking what might Nature permit you to do there? What will she not let you do; how might she help you out with your job? This is what true design is about – growing plants well in the right space. If you get the conversation right there will be a grace to your space, even if some of your combinations are a little unconventional.

Start with some idea of how you'd like the end result to look, trying to visualize how the overall garden will look when the plants are mature. First think about size (both height and spread). If you are planting an island bed then the largest plants should go in the middle, but if you are planting against a fence or wall, then keep tall plants to the back and short ones to the front. You need to think about the back, middle and front for light and shading reasons, but it's also important to break the rules. A tripod of beans near the front of a bed will not only make picking easier, it will add an air of mystery as you are forced to move through the garden to see what lies behind the beans. Sweetcorns are tall, but compact, so they can be dotted towards the front to add another dimension. Dill is tall, but so airy that it could be placed

A polyculture mix: to the rear, Jerusalem artichokes and 'Gardeners' Delight' tomatoes, Black Tuscan kale nestles among a pink Salvia and Primula denticulata to the front – the flowers are edible and attractive in salads.

goals. I like the lulls, the anticipation that comes with waiting for the next moment. Because edible landscaping is anticipating the rewards of food, I find the waiting all the sweeter. The garden changes all the time, there would be no point in creating a beautiful edible landscape that didn't get eaten just because it looked so pretty. This landscape is for eating and the design must pay heed to that.

There's a lot to be said for designing with straight lines. Traditional potagers with their parterres and endless geometric patterns are simple and pleasing, just paint in the numbers and colour between the lines. Polyculture is the Jackson Pollock of the design world, it weaves and splatters itself across the garden. There are moments of drama as one section bursts into flower, but the bold effect happens as each vegetable becomes ready to eat and patterns seem to appear from nowhere. It's like some wonderful buffet scattered across the garden as the edible world shows off its wares.

The crowning glory to all this in my garden is the apple tree at the end of the path. It's a Discovery apple, early, tasty enough (not my choice, but left by a previous owner) and festooned with bright red apples, the sort that a child might draw. As they ripen the garden goes from a hazy pink to hotter colours. Bright yellow patty pan summer squash and yellow courgettes appear, purple French beans begin to drip, chicory bursts

towards the front almost as a lace screen to look through. Play around a little, the joy of edible gardening is that most of the plants are in and out within the year – if something didn't work this year, there is always next. Each season, try to note what has worked (preferably with a picture), it's not only satisfying to look at on grey winter days, it helps with planning next year.

EVOLVING DESIGN

Nature moves, gardens evolve, everything changes. I have never understood gardens that try to stay the same, where constant perfection and perpetual flowering are the

into bright blue flowers and late summer spreads right across the garden.

There are some design imperatives. You need to be able to move in and out of your garden, and you need spaces to pick and harvest from, preferably without compacting the soil. A successful solution is to have stepping stones or keyhole paths where you can reach into a space and replant or harvest the latest crop. I use some square pavers that I had kicking around as stepping stones. I like them because they are not too heavy, so if I want to change positions they are easy to pick up and move elsewhere. If you're going to lay a path it is a good idea to dig out the valuable topsoil and replace it with some sort of hardcore, so that the path drains well and you make the most of the soil. My garden was once covered in gravel, I dug out a channel in the middle, raked all the gravel into this pit then laid reclaimed bricks on top to make a path. The spare soil went to raise the beds to the level of the path, and I now had a whole path to edge in pretty edible plants.

MAKING PLANS

When planning your garden, first map your permanent features – trees, bushes, shrubs, paths, and compost areas; the bits that are going to stay. Then think about the various layers, the colours, contrasts and forms you'll create across the spaces. Essentially you need three layers for ground cover, mid storey and height. Choosing wisely will mean you don't waste any space. The obvious pattern is to have ground-covering or low-growing plants at the front, mid storey in the middle and tall at the back, but I like to bring some tall to the front just to mess the rules about a bit. The main idea is to exploit all available spaces, there might be room for some low-growing, shade-loving herb under a tall bush. Or perhaps you could plant some bulbs underneath the fruit trees to make use of available spring light.

Playing around with colour is fun. My garden starts lemon yellow in spring, moves towards a girly pink, hazes into pastels before leaping into hot reds and purples and cool blues. You can get colour

SOME EDIBLES TO EDGE YOUR PATHS

Alpine strawberries.

Chives – thick bands of chives look spectacular in flower and garlic chives are a tasty alternative.

Parsley – curly is lower growing than Italian flat leaved, though both begin to peter out towards the end of summer.

Thyme, when clipped neatly into a low mound of a hedge is evergreen, looks wonderful in flower and is low maintenance if it likes your soil.

Marjoram or golden oregano is a good, very low-maintenance edging that appears all year round.

Salad bowl lettuce makes a lovely edging, but is difficult to keep going continuously all summer.

Edible edges: chives and mouse garlic edge the path.

into a vegetable garden by simply planting flowers around the vegetables, either edible flowers, flowers for cutting or just flowers that you love. Another way is to celebrate the flowers of vegetables. Those girly pinks in my garden come in part from potato flowers of 'Red Duke of York' and 'Maris Peer', the dusky pastels include the blues and pinks of mangetout pea flowers. Once no self-respecting seedsperson would bother to describe the flowers in a seed catalogue, but times are changing, particularly with the rise of patio gardens where the vegetables need to be both pretty and tasty.

Bright and arresting colours aren't everything, there is a corner of green under one of my apple trees that is completely delightful. It starts with a magnificent beast of a rhubarb and nestled around its base are three Mexican ground cherries with green husks that turn parchment brown by the end of the year. Next there is a weave of sweet cicely, with its soft fern-like foliage, then water mint, a mint blushed with purple, and herb chicory that bolts to the skies and festoons this green with sky blue flowers. These greens have depth and calm, and on the opposite side of the path is the bright-red apple and deep purples of perennial flowers and later purple sprouting broccoli.

I aim to make a tapestry out of my vegetables and flowers. Some of the simplest designs are strong contrasts, red and green lettuce grown in a weave down one edge of the garden, tall-growing plants with shorter ones, such as the sweetcorn and the ground cherries, or the contrast between forms, such as the strong upright growth of

purple sprouting broccoli nestled amongst white valerian flowers. When they work the garden looks seamless, and then the munch bunch come out to make tatters of leaves or one plant swamps another and you have to start unpicking the weave to where the problem lies and then pick up stitches again – sometimes it works, sometimes it doesn't. But one of the true joys of gardening is that there is always next year. I already have plans for what to move, and for other combinations that came too late to try this season, but I've pencilled them in for next.

THE JOYS OF COLOURS AND CONTRASTS

There's nothing dull about an edible garden, it can be as vibrant as any flowery patch, and

COLOURS AND CONTRASTS

BLUES AND GREYS

Kale 'Cavolo Nero' is a handsome, slate grey-blue.

Globe artichokes run almost silver.

Brussels sprouts can be a steely blue-green.

Peas are a vivid green with blue undertones.

Onions and garlic run a similar grey-blue, pale green gambit.

In winter, leeks take over the blue-green colour scheme.

GREENS

Most plants are green of sorts, but courgettes and winter and summer squashes have some of the most striking green leaves, partly due to their size.

The first stems of rhubarb may be blush pink or red, but the giant leaves are a satisfying green.

Swiss chard 'Fordham Giant' has white stems and deep green leaves.

Lovage is statuesque and a good green, but not one for small gardens.

There are dozens of green salads.

YELLOW, GOLD AND CREAM

Golden oregano is the easiest gold to work into the garden, followed by golden feverfew and the yellow splashes of variegated lemon balm.

'Austrian Yellow Leaf' lettuce is a pale buttery yellow.

Golden pea has bright yellow pods and yellow new shoots, though I think it looks a little more sickly than interesting.

Yellow peppers and chillies, yellow tomatoes, yellow courgettes and summer squashes.

Angelica turns a lovely buff yellow as it comes into seed.

Variegated land cress is splashed cream and green, varieties of variegated mints, sages and thymes run from silver to cream.

REDS, PINKS AND PURPLES

The deepest purple must belong to the lovely metallic leaves of the beetroot 'Bull's Blood'. 'Purple Orache' is a dusty version.

'Mascara', 'Lollo Rosso', 'Really Red', 'Devil Tongue' and 'Bresson Rouge' are some of the many purple lettuces.

Red Swiss chard, 'Rhubarb', 'Ruby' and the various forms in 'Bright Lights' are the best, brightest reds found in the vegetable garden, they are truly arresting when caught behind late afternoon light.

Tomatoes as they ripen on the bush are often a startling red, but can also be pink, yellow and orange.

Red Italian chicory brings reds into the winter, with 'Red Russian' kale and the curly kale 'Redbor'.

Purple kohl rabi is the smallest of the cabbage family, the huge purple heads of red cabbage are among the biggest.

Many Oriental vegetables are red and purple – giant 'Red Mustard', the beautiful dissected 'Red Frills' mustard and red pak choi and choy sum.

I blame my mother for my love of geraniums. They are not particularly useful but are very pretty and bring in lots of bees and beneficial insects.

there is also something to be said for those lush or quiet green corners. Play about with colour combinations, if they don't work for you try something else next time round.

If you have a wall behind your bed, one of the most simple and striking patterns is to plant some showstoppers at the back. A globe artichoke, towering Brussels sprouts, black Tuscan kale or a tower of beans will do the trick, surrounded by three or four bands of other plants. You could use chard around its base, then lettuce and to the front a low-growing herb, such as thyme. Bands of seedlings offer endless possibilities. Green and coloured lettuce and other salad crops can be nestled into spaces between other crops, providing a constantly changing palette of colours.

IN ORDER OF SIZE

Don't forget that the size of any plant will change over the seasons, so there will always be spaces to be exploited for a quick crop of lettuce or radishes, before a large annual plant, such as a courgette or giant sunflower, matures. But remember that large plants not only cast shade as they grow, they also demand more from the soil around them, particularly something fast-growing like a sunflower. For this reason there's no point trying to grow a sunflower and a parsnip together, both grow at roughly the same rate and will compete for moisture meaning one of the pair (most likely the parsnip) will suffer. Drifts are a real benefit in such spaces, such as a quick crop of baby salad leaves around the base of a sunflower as it's getting going – the leaves will be in and out before the sunflower really towers when it gets too tough for anything else to take up the ground space.

IN ORDER OF SIZE ...

FOR THE BACK

Jerusalem artichoke	Perennial	2m (6ft) tall
Globe artichoke	Perennial	1–1.2m tall x 1m wide (3 x 4ft)
Tree spinach	Annual	1.5m x 30cm (5ft x 12in)
Mountain orache	Annual	1.5m x 30cm (5ft x 12in)
Cardoon	Perennial	1.5 x 1.2m (5 x 4ft)
Cucumbers and climbing squashes up tripods	Annuals	From 1–2m tall (3–6ft)
Sweet peas, morning glories	Annuals	Climbing up tripods 2–3m (6–10ft)
Sweetcorn	Annual	1.5m (5ft)
Sunflowers	Annual	1.5–3.5m x 45cm (4ft 6in–12ft x 18in)
Courgettes	Annual	45 x 90cm (18in x 3ft)
Winter squash climbing up supports	Annual	1–1.5m (3–5ft)
Climbing beans	Annual	2m (6ft)
Climbing peas	Annual	1–1.5m (3–5ft)
Brussels sprouts	Annual	1m x 60cm+ (3 x 2ft)
Amaranthus caudatus	Annual	1m+ x 45–75cm (3ft+ x 2ft 6in)

IN THE MIDDLE

Bush courgettes	Annual	60cm x 45cm (2ft x 18in)
Asparagus	Perennial	1.5–2m x 30cm (5–6ft x 1ft)
Tomatoes	Annual	1–1.5m x 45–60cm (3–5ft x 18in–2ft)
Broad beans	Annual	1.2m x 30cm (4ft x 1ft) dwarf varieties 30 x 30cm (1ft x 1ft)
Potatoes	Annual	30–80cm x 60cm–1m (1–2½ft x 2–3ft)
Leeks	Annual	30–45 x 15cm (12–18 x 6in)
Kales	Annual	60 x 45cm (2ft x 18in) although 'black' kales can grow 2m (6ft) tall over two years
Swiss chard	Annual	30–40 x 30cm (12–15 x 12in)
Oriental mustards	Annual	20–40 x 30cm (8–15 x 12in)
Garlic	Annual	30–45 x 15cm (12–18 x 6in)
Cosmos	Annual	1m x 30cm (3ft x 12in)
Opium poppy		50cm x 20cm (20 x 8in)

TOWARDS THE FRONT

Beetroot	Annual	20–35 x 30–45cm (8–14 x 12–18in)
Carrots	Annual	20–30 x 15cm (8–12 x 6in)
Lettuce	Annual	20–30 x 10–35cm (8–12 x 4–14in)
Mizuna and mibuna	Annual	30 x 30cm (12 x 12in)
Rosette-forming pak choi	Annual	25–35 x 35cm (10–14 x 14in)
Chrysanthemum greens	Annual	15–50cm when flowering (6–20in)
Rocket	Annual	30–40cm (12–15in), in flower 60cm (2ft)
Wild rocket	Annual	25–35 x 30–45cm (10–14 x 12–18in)
Sorrel	Perennial	10–25cm tall (4–10in) in flower 50cm tall (20in)
Salsola	Annual	20–25 x 20cm (8–10 x 8in)
Shallots	Annual	25–30x 20cm (8–12 x 8in)
Sage	Perennial	25 x 30cm (8 x 12in)
Dwarf peas	Annual	20cm (8in)
Dwarf beans	Annual	20–40cm (8–16in)
Ornamental cabbages	Annual	45 x 25cm (18 x 10in)
Nemophila menziesii 'Penny Black'	Annual	20 x 30cm (8 x 12in)
Nicotiana x *sanderae* cultivars	Annual	30 x 45cm (12 x 18in)
Papaver nudicaule	Annual	40–50 x 15–20cm (15–20 x 6–8in)

RIGHT OUT ON THE EDGE

Wild strawberries	Perennial	10 x 15cm (4 x 6in)
Parsley	Annual	25 x 20cm (10 x 8in)
Chives	Perennial	30 x 30cm (12 x 12in)
Thymes	Perennial	10–20 x 30–45cm (4–8 x 12–18in)
Marjoram	Perennial	10–25 x 30cm (4–10 x 12in) 35–40cm (14–16in) when flowering
Land cress	Annual	10–20cm tall (4–8in) 35–40cm (14–16in) when flowering
Purslane	Annual	10–25 x 20cm (4–10 x 8in)
Pansies	Perennial	20–25 x 20–35cm (8–10 x 8–14in)
Violet	Perennial	10–20 x 20cm (4–8 x 8in)
Forget-me-nots		15 x 15cm (6 x 6in)

The Edible Directory

In order to design and eat well you need to know how you should grow each plant and what it needs to be happy.

PEAS AND BEANS

PEAS

I'm ambivalent about peas. Although fresh peas picked straight from the pod are gastronomic heaven (shelled seconds before cooking), growing enough to get from pod to pot seems near impossible, or at least difficult, unless you grow them traditionally with gaps between rows as wide as the height of the peas. Even then you need a lot to get a bowl full. Instead I grow one or two particularly beautiful varieties for their fine flowers and stick mainly to mangetout or sugar snap varieties for the pot. I grow masses for their pea tips in pots on the patio or kitchen windowsill.

There are shelling peas and mangetouts where you eat the whole pod – sugar snap are the American version where you let the pod swell slightly, but not past the point where they no longer snap when you break them in half. Varieties are broken down into early, middle and late. I mainly grow middle and late as I find the earlies difficult to keep happy as something else always wants to eat them.

Peas are large seeds so easy to sow. They need rich soil to do well. About five weeks into growth the nitrogen-fixing root nodules kick into action, but until then they need a good supply of food, home-made compost is definitely best. They don't like to dry out and need a good reserve of compost. I sow most of my peas in modules and plant them out, because I'm bored of battling with mice for the seeds when they're direct sown into the ground. A child's rubber snake or holly branches will deter some mice, but determined ones are another matter. Once the seed has started to germinate they are less interested and the pea can get on with growing.

Dwarf varieties such as 'Tom Thumb' don't give you much of a crop, but are so pretty to look at and perfect for patio planting to use as a living snack or nibbles for drinks. Semi-leafless types are pretty much all tendril and no leaf, they have compact growth,

Herb chicory in flower mingles with the South American vine Achocha, *whose young leaves and small cucumber fruit are both edible.*

Opposite: Pea 'Golden Sweet' – a beautifully ornamental pale golden pea.
Right: Broad bean 'Red Epicure' has crimson beans inside its pods.

a good habit and need no staking as they were bred for mechanical picking, so they're perfect for small spaces. Sadly they are pretty hard to get hold of so keep your eyes peeled in seed catalogues, especially for the best-known 'Sugar Crystal', and get your order in early.

Sowing peas

Sow peas from early spring for early summer pickings 2.5cm (1in) deep. Make the shape of the letter P with your hand (make a fist and stick out your thumb) this is the spacing needed between plants. Sow 'Sugar Ann' for mangetout and 'Kelvedon Wonder' for shelling. For main crops sow continuously – start the next crop as soon as the first is showing – until early summer. 'Oregon Sugar Snap' and 'Carouby de Mausanne' (oh so pretty) are good mangetout forms. For a truly weird form try 'Parsley Pea', a pea with parsley shaped tips for salads and peas for later picking.

Peas need support. The most naturalistic is twigs and brushwood, plastic netting is pedestrian, but purposeful. I make slightly eccentric homemade supports from *Cornus* and willow prunings. They look a little as if a drugged spider made them, but they work well and have a humour to them.

BROAD BEANS

Tender, thin-skinned broad beans make a mockery of the bitter, tough, shop-bought kind. The trick is to pick them young. You don't want beans more than 1.5cm (½in) long, which means picking young pods. If you pick the pods even smaller you can eat them whole, which is a lovely, if extravagant, treat and delicious in the Umbrian stew 'Scafata'.

Broad beans are not the easiest edible landscaping candidates, they can grow leggy and have a tendency to fall over, this is often quickly followed by an immense attack of blackfly. But given the right conditions and plenty of light to grow strong and upright they will reward you well with their chocolate-smelling flowers and handsome blue-grey leaves.

They are hardy souls, quite able to stand a long cold period. Traditionally they have been sown in autumn to harvest in spring, but although they can withstand a winter I've found it difficult to get a good crop from them. Mice often go for the beans and if you get a prolonged wet patch in autumn the beans rot off. I stick to an early module-sown crop that I plant out as fairly large plants. This works excellently as I can both keep mice at bay and ensure I get good upright growth by planting out larger plants, a must when you're trying to use broad beans as a stylish backdrop.

Broad beans need moist soil to go from their hard rustling seeds to tender young shoots, but if they have too much they'll turn to mush. You should water in well just after sowing and then leave them to it, don't water again until you see signs of life. Broad beans germinate at low temperatures, without any need for heat, but very cold, wet soil is not a good broad bean place. If you really like eating them try sowing in autumn and again in spring to have a long succession of cropping, but you'll need to experiment to find what suits you.

Sow seeds 5cm (2in) deep, roughly 20–25cm (8–10in) apart in both directions. Traditionally you plant in staggered rows, but I've had great success in drifts and patches. Dwarf forms, such as 'The Sutton', are less likely to flop around and good for smaller spaces. Much loved 'Aquadulce Claudia' is a bit of towering beast and needs support. I planted 'Red Epicure', gently pink-stained beans of medium height, this year and used pea sticks to support any flopping plants in a drift. It gave a lovely informal look, underplanted with an early, pink-flowering strawberry and bright green 'Eau de Cologne' mint wandering beneath the plants. The combination of blue-grey broad bean leaves, glossy mint and pink strawberry flowers was very pleasing.

FRENCH BEANS

I spend what seems like half the summer holding out for the first French beans, then, after a couple of weeks, I need very imaginative recipes to use up the glut that always appears. I wouldn't want it any other way. French beans are also known as kidney or haricot beans, so leave large ones on the plants and let them dry for a supply of winter beans. As they hail from South America they are tender and are sent straight to the ground come the first frost. For decorative purposes the prettiest must be the purple-podded beans, their flowers are violet, the stems dark purple and the beans are blushed purple when young, maturing to deep purple. Unfortunately they don't keep their colour when cooked.

French beans need a bit of cosseting. They like a sheltered, sunny spot and climbing forms need something to grow up. I sow indoors (or in a coldframe, depending on the weather) in late spring. They won't

> TIP
>
> Pinch out the top of the plant when it is fully in flower, as this concentrates the growth into producing beans and can help keep blackfly down. Don't drown blackfly in washing up liquid without hunting for ladybird larvae that may be around to control the bugs, as they'll die under a torrent of soapy liquid.

French bean 'Blauhilde' has tender purple beans.
Unfortunately they turn green when cooked.

DESIGN NOTE

Most of my climbing French beans are grown on tripods close to the path. There is little point in growing French beans at the back of border unless you've got easy access, as once they start fruiting you need to pick, pick, pick. If you give both plenty of space (use a spacious tripod) you can mix French beans with sweet peas or climbing nasturtiums. You can also try French beans climbing up sunflowers, but you have to grow the sunflowers in pots and give them at least a couple of feeds before planting them out with the beans. When it works it looks lovely. 'Borlotto Lingua di Fuoco', or 'Firetongue', has amazing pale green pods splashed violent red and filled with red and white beans that are excellent for drying. For several years I've grown 'Eva' for its exceptional flavour. 'Purple Podded' and 'Purple Queen' are equally good and highly decorative.

Runner bean 'White Emergo' produced plenty of beans all summer long from just four plants. Pick runner beans young as long ones become stringy.

germinate below 10°C (50°F) and there is no point sowing earlier as they can only be planted out after the last frost. You can sow them straight into the ground, but if conditions are the least bit wet the beans rot – and slugs love them. It's much better to raise them in large modules where you can plant out healthy young things that are already looking for something to start twining around.

I sow two batches, a dwarf variety to crop first and a climbing variety to extend the season. I leave about two weeks between sowing for a continuous crop. Dwarf beans are fast and attractive, they can be used to edge a bed and work well in pots. Slugs can be a nuisance as the pods tend to trail down to soil level, so you may want to give dwarf varieties something to support them, small twigs or other sturdy plants that won't mind being leaned on. Plants should be set about 20cm (8in) apart, but you can get away with planting them closer.

RUNNER BEANS

These beans also hail from South America and should be germinated like French beans. However runner beans like moisture-retentive, organic-rich soil and if they dry out in any way they won't produce. A good way of guaranteeing beans is to dig a trench where you're going to plant them out, and fill it with all sorts of semi-rotted food stuff and strips of newspaper. This acts as a moisture-rich slump for the beans to feed off.

You can direct sow the seeds (they're easier to get going than French beans), but I still rely on module-raised plants. Sow seeds in early spring indoors if it's cold. Germination is poor if temperatures are below 10°C (50°F). Plant out (or direct sow) towards the end of April, planting against strong cane supports 30cm (12in) apart. If you want a row to hide a hedge or a boundary wall, angle the canes towards the wall or hedge to make an 'A' frame so that the bean roots can grow well away from the dry conditions commonly found in such areas.

The flowers are pollinated by bees, which may not be busy if the weather is wet and cold. Flowers can also fail to set if there's a period of very hot weather with nights over 16°C (60°F). Some growers suggest spraying the flowers with water on hot days to help them set, I think a good soak at the base of the plant seems to do just as well. The more beans you pick the more you get. The beans should crop until the first frost, but it can be hard to manage to pick all the small and tender ones and they get stringy when they grow over 20cm (8in) long.

Cultivars

'Painted Lady' is the prettiest bicoloured, flowering red and pink. I have a soft spot for 'White Emergo', which has white and pale cream flowers. 'Scarlet Emperor' and the recently improved 'Scarlet Empress' are the most productive red-flowering varieties. Like French beans, you can grow them on tripods with sweet peas, as these come to an end the runner beans will continue to clamber over them.

Left: Blood sorrel or bloody dock has bitter leaves that can be used in salads or work well in omelettes. They are some of the first green leaves in spring.
Opposite: Beetroot 'Chioggia' is a pale beetroot with pink and white concentric rings that won't bleed when cooked.

ROOTS AND SHOOTS

BEETROOT

Some people still think of beetroot as a dull, rubbery, tasteless vegetable best eaten soaked in vinegar. To me it is a nascent, earthy vegetable that is sweet and tender. There's also a world of difference between shop bought and fresh garden beetroot where the sugars that make beetroot so delicious are still in place. I couldn't imagine my garden without a beetroot or my table without borscht.

Beetroot seeds are hardy, corky things that are actually clusters of seed that tend to germinate in little groups. These tough seeds need lots of moisture to get them going, so germination can be very slow in dry weather. This is one crop that is happiest sown direct; about 2cm (1in) deep, not right on the surface or they struggle to get their taproots down. Beetroot are tough enough to cope with most soils, though the roots can be small and skins tough on poor ground.

Small baby beets are ready in 9–12 weeks, larger ones 12–14 weeks. The baby leaves are great in salads, small beets delicious warmed with goats' cheese and larger ones perfect for soups. They store well in the ground and can be kept in place over a mild winter, but it is best to pull them up in autumn and store them somewhere dry, frost free and dark – a dustbin works well. To conserve moisture, store them in sand or old compost in a pot and place this in the dustbin.

To have a continuous supply, start sowing in early spring, as soon as the soil has warmed up to more than 7°C (44°F). You can keep sowing until midsummer, and at a push can make a last sowing at the end of July for winter supplies. Thin for mini beet 5cm (2in) apart, for larger beetroot 10–15cm (4–6in) apart.

'Bull's Blood' is the best looker, with deep red, shiny leaves and blood-red roots. It is good for making patterns with, they look wonderful against the pink flowers of Godetia, or among many annual flowers. 'Chioggia' is a heirloom variety from Italy that has concentric pink and white rings in the root, but fairly standard green leaves

Carrot 'Chantenay' is a shorter carrot suited to growing in pots.

so it looks prettier on the plate than in the garden. 'Boltardy' is a standard round red beetroot that is a very reliable cropper and stores well. The long tapered roots of 'Fornio' have distinctive flavour and store particularly well over winter.

BRUSSELS SPROUTS

Brussels sprouts are large plants for such tiny produce, so not in my top ten for a small garden, but they are one of the hardiest members of the cabbage family. The obvious bits to eat are the sprouts, which are actually tight leafy buds, but the sprout tops also make very good greens. If you want to grow them, stamp the ground down really firmly round their feet and don't dig the ground over before planting. They need a long growing season and should be sown in large modules from late winter to mid-spring, to give you crops from September to March. They need at least 60–75cm (24–30in) between plants and will eventually grow to over 1m (40in).

If you are planting Brussels amongst other plants you will need to make sure that they have enough room and won't be out-competed by other similar size plants, otherwise interplant them between established crops (I grow them between geraniums and mint). They can grow top heavy, so you will have to stake large plants to stop them rocking about, but other than keeping the butterflies off, they require little attention. If they seem a bit slow by mid season, give them a feed of organic liquid fertilizer.

As sprouts generally ripen from the bottom up, harvest from the bottom, eating the sprouting top last. Sometimes sprouts 'blow', opening up like a flower rather than keeping nice and tight. This is usually because of temperature fluctuations. You can still eat them, but use them as greens or in stir-fries.

CARROTS

Sweet, home-grown carrots are quite a thing. Steamed, sautéed, snacked on, they're a far cry from the large monsters offered in supermarkets.

Carrots need light, deep, stone-free, fertile open soil, which is quite a shopping list for many gardens. My way round the limitations of my ground is to grow baby carrots, or the shorter stumpy types, in containers on the patio, while I slowly build up fertility in the ground. A bonus is that container-grown carrots don't get hit by carrotfly as these insects fly very low and can't get to where I place my pots. I can't say I am self-sufficient in carrots, but I have enough to supply salads with some extra.

Carrot foliage is attractive, fine and fernlike, if you're sowing in the ground it lends itself well to being sown with hardy annuals. This can also help keep carrot fly at bay, as they get confused and can't find the carrots. You need to get the carrots:flowers ratio right though. I sow twice as many carrots to flowers and only choose airy annuals like love-in-a-mist, poppies or the flax, *Linum rubrum*. A sturdy subject, such as a marigold, will swamp the carrots. Although you can sow earlier, it's best to wait to sow carrots until the soil has warmed to 10°C (50°F). Early sowings will need to be covered with fleece until late spring. You will have to watch out for slugs that seem to find the carrots right after they've germinated, before they've even got going.

Large carrots should be thinned to 15cm (6in) apart, but for my small salad carrots I sow in drifts or fairly liberally across a pot and don't bother to thin. They muscle it out; the slugs get some, but most grow happily and offer tasty, finger-sized, sweet carrots.

Sow at two-week intervals from late spring until late summer. Maincrop (the large, straight sort) are sown from mid-spring to mid-summer, with the last harvest kept for storage over winter.

Carrot flies produce maggots that tunnel through carrots to make them inedible. You can tell if they're around because the carrot leaves turn red. Barriers, (fine horticulture fleece and annual flowers) will confuse and deter them, but the most important thing is not to thin when the weather is warm or windy as the fly is attracted by the smell of the plants and that is strongest when you're working with them. Thin on dull, still evenings and nip unwanted seedlings off at ground level rather than pulling them up.

My favourite varieties are 'Chantenay' (cone-shaped and good for storage), 'Parmex' (round stumpy type), 'Paris Market' (round type) and 'Ideal Red' (a mini carrot that is usually more red than orange).

CELERY

The easiest celery to grow in a small space is either self-blanching or leaf celery. Chinese celery, a hardy wild celery that is smaller than the supermarket type and has a hollow stem, and is good for flavouring stews and soups in winter, is another. Celery is worth

Garlic scape are unopened flowerheads that should be picked off the plant to improve the clove sizes. They are a delicacy, lovely briefly fried or steamed.

growing because it's so different from the supermarket stuff and packs quite a kick.

Celery germinates at 10°C (50°F), and should be started off inside, but not until mid spring, as seedlings will bolt if they spend more than 12 hours at temperatures beneath 10°C (50°F). Don't cover the seeds as celery needs light to germinate. Prick out seedlings into 9–15cm (4–6in) pots. Wait to plant out until there are five true leaves and all frost has passed. Celery is naturally found in marshy areas and needs a good supply of moisture and rich soil to get good crisp stems.

Self-blanching celery should be planted about 15–18cm (6–7in) apart, the wider apart they are, the thicker their stems will be. The most tender stems come from plants that are nestled up close to a neighbour, where less light gets to them. Self-blanching types need feeding and watering well to provide stems ready for cutting after 18 weeks. You can cut the whole plant out, but it's much better to cut individual stems.

Leaf celery is undemanding. Sow seeds from spring to late summer and space seedlings about 25cm (10in) apart in the ground. Once up, leaf celery can be cut frequently and will regrow. 'Parcel' has attractive, crinkly leaves. I've used it as a backdrop for more colourful vegetables and annual flowers, and run it like a ribbon through the centre of the garden. It makes surprisingly good cut foliage for flower arranging.

Black Tuscan kale, 'Cavolo Nero', is the mainstay of my garden, providing year round greens and looking mighty handsome with it.

GARLIC

Garlic is at the heart of my kitchen, so many of my dishes start with the fizzle of garlic going into hot oil. It's a simple crop to grow, requiring little other than good drainage and sun. It does best on rich soils, but will soldier through poor ones. There are only two requirements for a decent bulb. It must go through a cold period, at least a month below 10°C (50°F) and must have a long growing season. If it doesn't get the cold it means the bulb will not initiate properly or form cloves. The easiest way to please garlic is to plant it sometime between October and December, so it gets plenty of cool temperature growing before spring when it can mature and ripen ready for picking in July.

To plant garlic you carefully split the bulb and choose the plumpest cloves. Plant these 10cm (4in) deep, roughly 15cm (6in) from their nearest neighbours. When the leaves are up in spring you can maximize space and plant shallow-rooting flowers, such as violas or love-in-a-mist or dabs of lettuce leaves between the plants, but you mustn't completely swamp the garlic as it needs to bake a little. By the end of June the leaves should turn yellow and start to wilt, now the garlic is ready to be harvested. Bulbs need to dry before storage, preferably outside in sunny conditions, bring them indoors when they are completely dry.

If your soil is very wet and heavy plant cloves in large modules in autumn and keep them somewhere suitably cool like a coldframe (though watch out for mice) over winter. Plant the sprouted cloves in spring.

It's worth picking some of your garlic 'wet' in early summer, picking young immature bulbs that aren't yet fully separated into individual cloves. It has a wonderful mild, but nutty, flavour. I always plant extra specially for this. Occasionally some garlic will produce rather weird, curved flower spikes that don't tend to fully open, these are called scapes. The young, unopened flower head is a delicacy and particularly good in egg dishes. But in general don't let your garlic flower or your bulbs will be small.

Garlic divides into hard neck and soft neck. Soft neck garlic is the sort you find in shops, it's easy to grow and it stores well. Hard neck garlic is a fussier beast, but some say it has the best flavour. It needs free-draining soil, tends to run to flower and doesn't store well. 'Cristo', 'Arno' and 'Thermidrome' all work well for me planted in autumn. It is possible to plant 'Solent Wight' in spring, although you tend to get smaller cloves, but it's worth planting some in spring to harvest wet in summer.

KALES

Kales are good landscaping plants, from the deeply crinkled leaves of curly kale to long, thin black Tuscan kales and giant 'Red Russian'. I have used the black Tuscan 'Cavolo Nero' dotted about near the back of the border as a brilliant foil for other colours and textures and the intensely red 'Red Russian' or the F1 'Redbor' to take the garden from summer into winter.

One of my favourite members of the cabbage family, kales are pretty low maintenance, apart from keeping pigeons and butterflies at bay. They're quick and easy to germinate, with no need of heat. I sow in modules that allow me to plant out healthy specimens wherever I see fit, they do best in fairly rich soil with very good drainage. Sow in mid to late spring for an autumn and winter supply, and very early spring for a summer supply. The black Tuscans are short-lived perennials and will happily go from a late spring sowing into the next year and on, though they tend to get taller and leggier. The red kales get prettier the colder it gets as their pink, red and purple tints come out with the frosts. If left to flower they will self-seed freely, which is one way to get a wonderfully informal look the following year.

Kales are large plants and will need at least a 30–40cm (12–16in) growing space. They will inevitably shade whatever is around them, particularly the broadleaf types, so they mix best with vegetables that don't mind a bit of shade, such as Swiss chard or peas that like shade around their feet and grow to find the sun. They can become top heavy so mound up the soil around their bases to stop them toppling over, and don't cut the whole plant down when you harvest or it takes ages to come back. Instead, take a few leaves from different plants and discard the bottom leaves every now and again, as the middle leaves are the tastiest.

Watch out for slugs at the early vulnerable stages, once kales get going they can withstand a lot of nibbling, and pick off caterpillars as you see them. One good way to find the large white caterpillar, which is a perfectly camouflaged green, is to look for their black poo (or frass) that accumulates at the base of each leaf, then work upwards inspecting every corner of the leaf to find the caterpillar. Chickens love the green caterpillars that turn into large white butterflies and hate the yellow, white, green and black ones that turn into

small whites. Fine mesh or fleece is a good way to keep caterpillars at bay, but it doesn't look pretty.

Kales make good container specimens and look lovely come winter with violas around their base. You can grow all kales as cut-and-come-again crops, sowing seeds thinly in wide drifts (or across a large pot) and cropping at 5–10cm (2–4in) high. They are relatively slow-growing, but will reflush with growth at least two or three times. Sow from early spring to late summer.

The blue-green foliage of many kales goes well with hot, strong colours, such as pink *Lychnis coronaria*, the salvia 'Pink Perfection' and red and purple shades of opium poppies *Papaver somniferum*.

KOHL RABI

Kohl rabi is another member of the cabbage family. I have a love-hate relationship with the cabbage family. I love sprouting broccoli and kales, but cabbages, Brussels sprouts and cauliflowers seem rather a lot of hassle with their lengthy growing periods, their demands for space and tendency to be nibbled before you get to them. Kohl rabi is the opposite to all of this. It's quick, small, tasty, drought and heat tolerant and not around long enough to attract any unwanted guests.

The stem of kohl rabi swells into a tasty bulb that should be eaten by the time it's about the size of a tennis ball. You can also eat the leaves. Plants mature within 8–10 weeks, so it's a good catch crop for in-between spaces. You can sow from early spring in modules indoors, planting out six weeks later, once the frost has passed, or you can sow outside until late summer, although the later crops will need cover if you want to harvest in early winter. Over-crowding checks growth so thin well and allow 20cm (8in) between plants for large varieties and 10cm (4in) or less for smaller varieties.

You need to cook the leaves and stems separately. I like to pick mine golf ball size. Boil them until tender, peel and smother in butter and a little grainy mustard. They are also good peeled and grated in salads. Watch out for pigeons, I find upturned hanging baskets make good barriers, and there are usually plenty of those in skips.

Kohl rabi are small enough to come to the front of the border. Both purple and green forms have greyish-green foliage, and I have enjoyed them planted towards the front of a bed with old-fashioned pinks.

LEEKS

Traditional big leeks need a long growing season, you start sowing in spring and don't harvest until early autumn. Leeks germinate at between 10–15°C (50–60°F), so in order to get this long season you should sow indoors in late winter or early spring. You can sow in batches in modules, or plant out as large plugs (the thickness of a pencil) spacing them 25cm (10in) each way. Small leeks, however, are much quicker to produce, often tastier and far less demanding. Sow mid-spring in batches until mid-summer (mid-July is the cut off point), either directly in drifts, or in modules to plant out when the leeks are large enough to handle. Start pulling them when they are pencil-sized or leave them to grow just that bit thicker. They will happily stand over winter if you throw fleece over them as protection from the worst frosts.

Rust can be a problem on leeks, there is little you can do about it and it will lower yields, though the plants remain edible. 'Pandora' shows a degree of resistance to rust and is good for mini leek production. It has lovely blue-green foliage and looks wonderful left to over winter and stand with the tulips.

ORACHES (*ATRIPLEX HORTENSIS*)

Oraches, sometimes known as mountain spinach, are one of the oldest-known food crops. Here, they're more likely to be grown as an ornamental than a food crop, which is all good for the edible gardener. Orache tastes a little like mild spinach, but is much easier to grow as it can withstand high temperatures. Once it's established in your garden, nature will take care of seed production and if orache is happy it will

Young leaves of red orache are an excellent spinach substitute.

stay forever. Ornamental growers often grumble about this, but if you see weeding as harvesting then it is no hardship.

There are three oraches – light yellow, deep green and red. The red is a showstopper, growing to more than 2m (6ft) and turning a brilliant buff-colour in late autumn festooned in thousands of seeds. It doesn't lose its colour when cooked, which makes for interesting looking omelettes! The leaves from young plants are best to eat as they're tough and inedible once the orache decides to bolt. Nip out the tip when the plant is about 10cm (4in) tall to make it bush out and produce more small leaves.

GIANT SPINACH OR TREE SPINACH (*CHENOPODIUM GIGANTEUM* 'MAGENTASPREEN')

Tree spinach seems to have suffered the same fate as orache. It's astonishing that it is so little known when it looks so extraordinary. Much like orache, it bolts to the skies come mid summer, but unlike orache you can carry on picking the leaves. It's a giant form of the edible weed 'fat hen'. Tree spinach looks a bit like 80s clubbing wear, but in a good way. The leaves are brilliant green with a light dusting of 'flour' over the surface, the undersides and the very young leaves are brilliant magenta pink. Young leaves can be eaten raw and larger, older ones cooked just like spinach.

Once established it seeds itself around a lot, but I had some trouble getting it going from direct sowing in my garden. I think the young seedlings need a lot of light and

were quickly out-competed by other plants. Raising in modules sown in spring seems the best approach, spacing seedlings about 25cm (10in) apart. Start to harvest at 10cm (4in) high and leave the ones at the back of the border to go to seed.

ORIENTAL GREENS

Oriental greens are a large, loose group of largely mustards and other brassicas that come from Asia (mainly China and Japan). They make great salad and stir-fry crops that you sow in late summer and harvest into the autumn and beyond. Or sow in early spring for delicious baby-leaf crops, summer-sown crops tend to run to seed very quickly though. Although they need warm temperatures to produce abundant leaves rather than stems, they will withstand long periods of cold.

Oriental greens include pak choi, rosette-forming pak choi (also sold as tatsoi), choy sum, which is like pak choi with an edible flower stem, mizuna, which has serrated leaves, mibuna with paddle-shaped leaves, the very hardy komastuma greens that are somewhere between mustards and turnip leaves, and mustard greens, including the pretty frilly sorts and Chinese cabbage. I've found this last one the hardest to grow as it needs heat to start, is munched to death by slugs and bolts at any sign of discomfort (but it might just be your thing).

One of the joys of Oriental greens is that many have a touch of heat, so they are generally left alone by slugs. However, flea beetle can be a problem in late summer, peppering the leaves with small holes. The only way to combat this is to cover the crop after sowing with a fine mesh or fleece to keep the beetles out. There is no point covering the crop once it is up as this just traps the bugs in.

Pak choi, choy sum and tatsoi are fleshy and mild, mizuna, mibuna and mipoona (a cross between the two) are also mild, but as the plants mature the leaves become tougher. The mustards are hot, and though this heat tastes spicy at the beginning of the season, by the end it's mind-blowing. Once the heat sets in don't use them in salads, but cook them very quickly in stir-fries or wilt in boiling water – a quick dunk in rapidly boiling water or a swirl around a very hot frying pan does the trick. Joy Larkcom recommends the cool of pak choi, stir-fried with the heat of a mustard and some garlic and fresh ginger as the perfect introduction to how good these vegetables can taste.

Many seed companies offer a 'spicy salad mix' or 'Oriental stir-fry greens mix' as an introduction. They are good for using as baby leaves for salads, but it's hard to get a satisfactory mix as each plant grows at such different rates. They do look lovely and wild growing in a pot, but if you're at all serious about trying out this world of vegetables it is better to grow the individuals separately. The many F1 hybrids all tend to mature at the same time and I have been left baffled by what I am going to do with 20 pak choi all ready to be picked! Sow 'Green Revolution' or 'Red Choi' in small batches several days apart to get around this.

Some are stunning landscaping plants. Mustard 'Giant Red' has large deep green leaves touched with red that turns maroony purple as cold nights appear. It grows up to 60cm (2ft) tall and at least 20cm (8in) wide. Plants need to be spaced 30–40cm (12–16in) apart and make a good

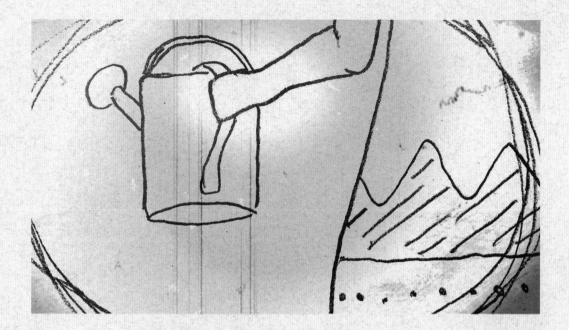

ribbon running through the middle of a border. Green-in-the-snow mustards are the hardiest, they have dark green leaves with ragged edges and come into their own in winter when their deep green leaves look so healthy while everything else sleeps. Try intercropping these between the red mustards.

Frilly-leaved, winter-hardy mustards include 'Art Green' and 'Green Wave'. They're quite a sight surrounded by a ring of winter violas or edging a bed. Deeply dissected forms include 'Green Frills', 'Red Frills' (deep reddish-purple) and 'Golden Streaks' (pale yellow-green). They are not only both decorative, but they also keep me in greens for the winter, so they're indispensable. Sow them in late summer and space 20cm (8in) apart, although they can be grown much closer together in pots and treated much like a cut-and-come-again salad. All winter-hardy Oriental greens can be used as a backdrop of colour to winter bedding, such as pansies, violas and double daisies like the 'Bellissimo' series.

PARSNIPS

You don't think much of parsnips when the garden is in full summer flower, but come winter the rich sweet flavour of these roots make them a failsafe soup for long winter nights or an indulgent crisp. My favourite way to eat them is slow roasted with salt, a little rosemary, perhaps some carrots and then dipped in tomato ketchup – trashy carbohydrate heaven.

To get long, thick roots you need a long growing season. Parsnip seed also needs a long germination period in damp soil. I think it's best to sow in late spring or early summer in the ground, but unless you mark seed it's easy to forget where they are. The old trick is to sow radish in between your parsnips, or try mixing them with annual flowers and sowing them altogether in a drift, thinning as necessary. Parsnips should be 20cm (8in) from their neighbours, but I tend to space them a bit closer and grow mini-parsnips, which are pulled when thumb-sized, very good for roasting and much easier for heavy or very shallow soils.

'Salad Blue' potato is a waxy potato with purple skin and insides. It looks lovely in salads.

Harvest parsnips from autumn into winter, many people swear they taste better after a frost. It is a good idea to chuck bracken, bushy twigs or straw over the foliage so that the ground does not completely freeze (and it helps you find them on dark evenings). If you let a couple go to seed in spring they are quite dramatic, very tall and loved by hoverflies.

'Gladiator' and 'Avonresister' are firm favourites. Sow with love-in-a-mist, poppies or marigolds. I've also had some success with weaving the golden mustard 'Golden Streaks' between plants, it complements the dark green parsnip foliage.

POTATOES

From my childhood onwards eating new potatoes swirled in butter, dripping in French dressing, or dusted in paprika and salt, meant summer was here.

Potatoes, for me, mean small new ones, often rare or hard to find varieties, but rarely large maincrops. I have little desire to grow large floury potatoes. I'll leave that to the farmer who has space, and that's my recommendation to the back garden grower. You need a lot space to be self-sufficient in potatoes and although I think that they are more handsome a crop than people realise, I don't think it's worth digging up your garden to grow enough to keep you in spuds year round. Grow some earlies for their fantastic flavour and stop there.

I put at least ten plants into my garden last year, partly to do some free digging on my behalf to break up the ground, and partly as a measure of my soil quality. The results are better than I expected, no scab and little sign of eelworm (a small, dreaded thing that affects yields and quality). Potatoes are not easy to design with, they do have pretty flowers, but just as they are beginning to look magnificent they flop all over their neighbours. You can't grow them in the same place two years running, and you can't move them from back to front because of their size, so I think the best way to grow potatoes is in a field, or in a pot.

Pot-grown potatoes are fantastic. The floppy growth that's difficult to work with in the garden is fine in a pot, and potatoes are large enough to mask ugly walls and less attractive spaces. They need little attention, other than watering and good compost, and you get such great rewards – when you knock over the pot to expose those lovely tatties it feels a bit like mining for gold, hunting through the compost to find the bounty. A healthy plant will produce about 15 potatoes of varying size. I grow two or three plants per 90-litre pot (dustbin sized). Five pots provide plenty of potatoes to keep me going through the summer.

Which potato to grow?

Early potatoes take roughly 90 days to mature, and second earlies take 110 days. Some very fast growing ones, such as 'Swift' are called very early earlies and they're ready in 75 days. First and second earlies are less likely to get blight than maincrops. I favour waxy ones with very low dry matter – you can see a pale slick of oil when you cut through them raw. This means when they are cooked they remain intact, making them perfect for salads.

I grow the majority of my potatoes in pots on the patio and get excellent results.

HOW TO GROW POTATOES IN A POT

I always buy good-quality seed potatoes in January, mostly from Potato Days. I don't see much point in chitting them (the process of starting tubers off indoors to get an earlier crop), which is often at the expense of overall yield. You allow the potatoes to sprout somewhere bright, but cool, and once the sprouts are 2.5cm (1in) long and the soil is warm enough out they go. I don't chit because it is very easy to get the whole process wrong. The tubers can easily dry out, the fragile sprouts can

be broken and if you are planting into soil that's too dry, too wet or too sticky, or if heavy frost appears, you can't plant out or the sprouts will be damaged. I think most people chit just because they like to see something growing at that time of year. Instead, I keep my potatoes somewhere cool, frost-free and dark to stop them from sprouting. I plant in mid-March, technically the soil needs to be 6°C (43°F), placing 25 litres of compost in the bottom of a pot and nuzzling three equally spaced potatoes about 5cm (2in) beneath the surface of the compost.

As the potatoes sprout and grow I cover the new shoots with more compost until I reach the top of the pot. This encourages the plant to produce tubers throughout the whole pot and seems to give a bigger crop

A NOTE ON POTATO BLIGHT

The same blight that affects tomatoes affects potatoes. As the disease doesn't usually appear until mid to late summer, growing first and second earlies is a good policy, as they'll be dug out before the blight. If you want to grow maincrop potatoes, 'Sarpo Miro' and 'Sarpo Axona' are blight-resistant cultivars. You should cut the foliage down (whether it has blight or not) in August to stop the potatoes getting too big. Potatoes infected with blight are still edible if you get to them quickly enough, but they don't store. Burn or bag any infected leaves or stems.

than just planting the seed potatoes in the middle of a pot of compost.

Potatoes in pots won't need food if you're using good-quality compost (mix in a little of your own homemade for good measure), but they will need water – a good long soak once a week is more useful then just a daily sprinkle. Slugs can and will attack the foliage, particularly in warm, wet summers, even stripping a plant down to its midrib. Deal with them before the problem gets out of hand.

RADDICHIO OR RED CHICORY

Chicories are a large group of edible biennials and perennials. They are most confusing because depending on where you live you either call them raddichios, chicory or endives (which is actually a separate species, *Chichorium endivia*). Most green chicories ('Belgian', 'Witloof' or 'Sugar Loaf') and most endives are only truly tasty when blanched (grown in the dark) to remove the bitterness. This is not necessary for raddichio as the cold usually takes the extreme bitterness out of them.

I only grow raddichio because they are the easiest to grow and because I once fell in love with an Italian (disastrous affair, but I did learn a lot about food) who made the most wonderful risotto out of 'Rossa Bella' raddichio swirled in at the last minute. Excuse my bias but if you want to learn about blanching chicories Joy Larkcom's *The Vegetable Garden Displayed* is the place to look.

Raddichio is equally good as a winter salad or cooked – leaves are bitter in summer and they need cold weather to mellow the flavour. They are beautiful plants, always showing some red, and are often variegated or splashed with white and vibrant greens. No winter edible garden should be without a strand or two of the incredibly hardy 'Red Treviso', although other varieties will need to be grown under some sort of cover if you want to pick all winter long. The flavour gets better as the weather gets colder. Either pick individual leaves or cut the whole head, in mild winters the stumps will resprout providing smaller leaves that are ideal for salads.

Chicories will grow in most soils, but prefer it well-drained and fairly rich. Sow in late June for an autumn crop (wait until the first frost before picking) and in August for a winter crop. I sow cold-hardy Italian varieties in August and cover if needed during the winter. Sow either in the ground or in modules or seed trays, spacing the plants 25–30cm (10–12in) apart. I think

that mature plants need to be snuggled up quite tight as neighbours can provide a degree of shelter from truly bad frost (which will blacken the leaves, but not kill them). You can pack straw between plants or cover them with fleece or tunnels. Check winter plants regularly for decaying leaves, as plants can rot in wet winter. Once the slugs have disappeared due to the cold, not much will bother raddichios.

The best red cultivars come from Italy, where raddichio growing is taken so seriously that the names of regional forms are controlled much like Champagne.

Compact varieties for smaller spaces include upright 'Rossa di Treviso', a red and white striped form from northwest Italy. 'Rossa di Treviso Tardiva' is a new very frost resistant variety that you can harvest till March. 'Verona Palla Rossa' is another hardy version that forms a large round head and needs cold temperatures to turn really red.

SHALLOTS AND ONIONS

To grow enough onions to keep me supplied would take up too much of my garden. I have tried to sneak onions into various places, to play around with spacing and intercropping, but onions need sun and very little competition to be happy. Even weeds are too much for most onions to cope with. If you buy sets (small onions ready for planting) in spring then onions are a doddle to grow, but you do need dedicated space. So I don't grow onions in general but I save a little space for autumn-planted Japanese overwintering onions. I

love the traditional 'Sensyu' yellow onions and make room for just enough to take me from late spring to summer. These don't store but they do give us lovely fresh onions (greens and all) for summer salads. Plant these out in autumn roughly 15cm (6in) apart in bare soil. Cover with pea sticks to keep the birds off until they start to put their roots down.

I think shallots are worth making room for. They do need light, space and weed-free soil to grow in, but you can get hold of very unusual shallots that you'd never find in a supermarket, including French banana-shaped shallots and red-skinned varieties that taste really good in salads. Look for the firmest shallots (bigger doesn't necessarily mean better) and plant them up to their necks in good, weed-free soil. You'll need to protect them from birds that will want to dislodge them until they get their roots down, but that's about it. They need plenty of light, so don't plant anything too close to them.

SWISS CHARD

Swiss chard can be fiendishly expensive in shops, but is easy to grow and as pretty as a picture in the ground or in pots. In fact it's almost too pretty, the variety 'Bright Lights' (with stems and midribs all brilliant hues of pink, yellow, orange and red) is fast becoming an edible landscaping cliché, but it is a real joy to see those brilliant stems caught in slanting, late autumn light and they're even better in the pot. Swiss chard is very good for the neglectful veg gardener as it seems to withstand a lot of abuse. It's rarely attacked by pests other than a leaf miner that appears sporadically throughout the summer to blister leaves. You should remove and bin

Tiny shallots grown for preserving. I pickled this lot whole and they made a delicious sweeter alternative to silver-skinned onions.

them as your compost won't get hot enough to kill the pests.

The seed is similar to the closely related beetroot, small clusters of hardy corky seed. You can sow in seed trays and prick out into modules, but it's perfectly suited to sowing outside in the ground. It will tolerate some shade and its deep roots mean it can tolerate drought so they need a deep container.

Sow in late spring for summer and autumn pickings, and in mid to late summer for late autumn and (if the weather is kind) winter picking. White varieties such as 'Fordham Giant', seem hardiest. Plants need to be spaced about 40cm (16in) apart to get big, handsome specimens, they'll be smaller if you sow closer. If you love the slightly nutty stems you should grow big plants, if you're more interested in the leaves, smaller plants with less midrib will suit you.

If sown too early, chard will quickly run to seed, but as the plants look amazing in flower, let them go if you have the space or cut back flowering shoots to encourage further pickings of small leaves. 'Ruby Chard' and 'Rhubarb Chard' are particularly prone to bolting, the white forms may look less interesting, but they're most productive. 'Fordham Giant' is particularly vigorous and shade-tolerant, I'm growing mine beneath a large rose bush and the white stems draw light into this shady spot, by autumn they are surrounded by *Cyclamen coum* and autumn-flowering crocus, when their white midribs suddenly look very stylish.

The white varieties also seem happy enough to sit around in modules until a place become available, which makes them a useful back-up plant. I always try to have some spares kicking around for

those times when the slugs or something else has got one crop and there is a horrible bare spot. They quickly grow away into their new home.

If you're plagued by pigeons you'll need to use netting or bird scarers to keep the birds off the leaves, or they'll decimate them. If they can sit on the netting and peck through they will, so be inventive.

CHRYSANTHEMUM GREENS (CHOP SUEY GREENS)

These are edible chrysanthemums, grown for their leaves and edible petals for use in stews and soups. The clear yellow petals with egg yolk centres are delightful in autumn and are much visited by bees and other insects. The petals look brilliant strewn across soups. They are unfussy about soil types and just need sun. To harvest enough leaves you have to keep cutting back the plant, but I love the blooms so I always let some flower. The flavour of the leaf is rather bitter and an acquired taste that gets more pronounced in hot weather or older plants.

Sow the seed on the surface of your soil, pressing it down into the compost rather than burying it. Sow from early spring to early summer, and again in late summer to early autumn. My plants liberally self-sow. You can start cutting after six weeks when the plants are around 15cm (6in) high. I don't much worry about spacing, but around 7–15cm (3–6in) apart is best for bushy growth. The more you pinch out, the more sideshoots you get. As plants get older the stems become too tough to eat, but you can strip off the sideshoots.

SALSOLA

Otherwise called land seaweed, this is a salt marsh plant adapted to grow in water and soil with high levels of salt. It stores the salt in its leaves, so it's a naturally seasoned plant. It can be eaten raw in salads or lightly boiled for no more that 30 seconds, so it remains crunchy, tastes salty and looks a brilliant green – quite the side dish. It prefers warmer conditions in full sun, but grows well in poor soil. I sow in late spring to early summer and although some seed packets suggest that it germinates best in low temperatures, I find a little heat works wonders. I sow in modules and raise the plants in 15cm (6in) pots until they are big enough to go out. It can be harvested as soon as it is around 5–10cm (2–4in) tall. The more you harvest, the more it branches out. I space my plants around 10cm (4in) apart or dot them in sunny spots along the edge of the path.

SALADS

LETTUCE

Lettuce is a big deal in my garden. I love to eat huge bowls of salad pretty much every day. I grow cut-and-come-again salads to harvest as young leaves in containers on the patio, as close to the kitchen as possible, and full heads of lettuce in the garden that I either harvest leaf by leaf or as a whole plant if it's a hearting type. I'm very particular about which varieties make it into the garden, allowing only beautiful lettuces that I can create patterns with and weave in and out of the front of the border.

The best way to make sure you have a continuous supply of lettuce is to grow your next crop in modules and have these standing by. As soon as you harvest one head, replace it immediately with a younger plant. This not only means a constant supply for the kitchen, but no great gaping holes in the garden.

CUT-AND-COME-AGAIN SALAD LEAVES

Cut-and-come-again is a Joy Larkcom special (see Resources page 251) where you grow lettuces very close together – no more than 2.5cm (1in) apart – and cut leaves when they're about 10–15cm (4–6in) high, essentially harvesting a lot of baby leaves. You can grow any lettuce this way, but the best are loose-leaf types that form loose tufts of leaves. They're productive, vigorous and slow to bolt and only take between four and six weeks from sowing to first cropping. A block of these can give you weeks, even months of supply.

Catalogna types have long, thin, arrow-shaped leaves that are highly attractive and very hardy. Lollo types, typified by the red 'Lollo Rosso', are super curly, almost frizzy, lettuces that possibly look better than they taste, but make good edgers. Specific 'Salad Bowl' cultivars come in a variety of reds and greens and often look like oak leaves, they wilt quickly after picking, but their soft texture makes for a great salad.

Hearting (heading) types

Hearting lettuce take from 12 to 18 weeks to mature and need to be spaced around 25–30cm (10–12in) apart to grow into good heads. If they're grown too close together they can tend to bolt. Butterheads or Roundheads are soft, cabbage-shaped lettuces with good flavour. Fast growing and quick to bolt when the weather is hot, they're best grown at the beginning and end of the season. Crispheads are either dull 'Icebergs' or lovely 'Batavian' types that are as crisp as an 'Iceberg', as flavoursome as a 'Butterhead' and delightful to look at. 'Cos' or 'Romaine' is the lettuce of Caesar salads, a crisp, upright, relatively hardy lettuce with a sweet flavour. Semi-Cos is the 'Little Gem' lettuce, very good for small gardens and you get the best of both worlds, a sweet heart and some looser leaves around the edges.

WHEN TO SOW

Lettuce germinates at relatively low temperatures, so start sowing as soon as spring gets going and sow right through until September, though by midsummer

Everything nibbled, nothing devoured: 'Flashy Butter Oak' and 'Australian Yellow Leaf' lettuce, with fennel, violas, runner beans and chives.

germination becomes erratic and temperatures over 25°C (77°F) mean you're in trouble. There is a critical couple of hours, just after germination, when it's curtains if the temperature fluctuates too high. If the weather is warm, sow in the evening or sow somewhere shady in a cool corner, bringing them out once you see green emerging. Hot summer temperatures also cause premature bolting and though lettuce looks great then, it tastes horrible, very bitter. You can tell when a lettuce is about to bolt as the leaves exude a white sap when snapped off. This is the start of a chemical process to start seed production, the bitter white sap works as pest control, you'll never find a slug on a bolting lettuce, so next year's seeds are protected.

A good rule of thumb is to sow little and often, start sowing the next crop once the first one is up, but come September you need to sow winter varieties that will need some sort of protection from bad weather. It is entirely possible to eat lettuce all year round in a cool climate. I sow up to mid October and I eat the last sowings at the end of April, which gives you an idea of how winter slows things down. After that, if I need a quick crop it happens on the kitchen windowsill as microgreens.

I tend to germinate all my lettuce in seed trays and then prick them out into modules. Although this is a little time-consuming it makes for good strong plants that tend to be more resilient to pests and diseases, particularly slugs. All too often I have found lettuce sown in the ground succumbs too easily to slugs. Lettuce will quickly form a blanket across the soil, keeping weeds down and, as my mother, says 'they are happiest when they can rub shoulders with each other'. Small cultivars need to be 15–20cm (6–8in) apart, large ones 30–35cm (12–14in) apart. They make good companions for sweetcorn, garlic and other tall slow-growing crops where they can create a living mulch around their feet. This year I experimented with lettuce and courgettes, growing a red looseleaf type in a wave below a young courgette. As the courgette grew it threw valuable shade onto the lettuce and neither seemed bothered by their slightly cramped conditions.

Healthy lettuce need a good supply of nutrients and moisture. In dry weather, water well. There is a critical period about a week before maturity when the plant bolts or becomes bitter if it doesn't get water. Tender lettuce leaves are manna to slugs, which will make their way very quickly through a crop, so be vigilant. Beer traps (or brewers yeast, orange juice, coke or anything sweet and smelly) will destroy a fair few, organic slug pellets are useful but still chemical, nightly slug hunts with a torch, frogs, hedgehogs, ducks and used coffee grounds will all help to keep the population down, but ultimately the best defence is a healthy plant on good soil. They can and will grow out of a lot of damage, but only if they are fighting fit.

OTHER SALAD LEAVES

You know you've become a great salad grower when people start picking through your salads, not to look for slugs, but because there are so many interesting flavours. The great gardener Beth Chatto once told me that she didn't think it was right to serve up a salad with less than 14 different ingredients, and I can finally say I agree.

LANDCRESS

Landcress is watercress for the streamless, with exactly the same peppery bite as watercress. It is a low-growing salad that is best grown in the autumn for winter pickings, by spring it has gone to seed. If you're lucky it will self-seed round your garden to provide a possible year-round supply. It makes a useful front of border

Alfalfa sprouts are a good fall back between hungry gaps. Sprouted in water, they take 2–6 days before they are ready.

plant and is a saviour for winter salads, or cooked like watercress.

You can grow it without protection in winter, but leaves can get a bit tough whereas you'll get lovely large, tender leaves under fleece or clear plastic. Leaves can be harvested roughly eight weeks after sowing from midsummer to early autumn. It's a good one for sowing direct in drifts, with plants thinned to about 15cm (6in) apart. It likes moist soil, but doesn't mind semi-shade so can be established under larger plants. It will bolt or become very tough if the soil dries out. I've grown very successful crops in wooden boxes, but you do need to water a lot. Landcress is lovely when it flowers, especially the variegated form with bright yellow flowers and white and green foliage.

ROCKET

There are two types of rocket, wild and cultivated. Both now grow wild in my garden. Wild rocket has smaller, stronger-flavoured leaves and is a slower growing perennial plant so a very useful, low-maintenance salad choice. I'm not sure how rocket got its name, but it certainly grows fast. In the right conditions, say in mid spring, you can be picking leaves three to four weeks after sowing.

Rocket will withstand light frosts and, though it runs to seed in very hot weather, the flowers are delicious and look lovely in salads, as well as attracting hoverflies and other beneficial insects. Rocket is pretty tolerant of most conditions, my

plants have self-seeded all over the place and I see weeding them out as part of my salad harvesting. Individual plants should, theoretically, be thinned to 15cm (6in) apart, but they can grow much closer together. Sow from midwinter under a cloche or direct into pots on the ground from early spring to autumn. They will get very established under brassica crops. Flea beetle can be a problem in midsummer, either cover seedlings with a fine mesh or sow in early spring and again in late summer and early autumn to avoid the problem.

PURSLANE

Also known as claytonia or miner's lettuce, purslane is a fleshy, paddle-shaped salad plant with pretty, small, white flowers. It grows slowly throughout the winter and can be be picked in early spring when there is little else about. It's another self-seeder that appears all over the garden once established, then you get to harvest odd volunteers all year round. It does best on lighter soils, but you can establish it pretty much anywhere, including in light shade, as long as there is good drainage. All parts are edible when young; as the plant matures eat only the leaves. Sow from early to late spring in the ground, then at any time until autumn. If it self-seeds, transplant volunteers to form clumps where you want them (chickens love it).

CORN SALAD

Lambs lettuce, corn salad or mâche is another winter salad that tastes distinctly of corn. It is a little bland on its own, but very good with sharp cheese and fruit. It is very low-growing with small leaves, best sown in late summer or early autumn for winter use as it tends to bolt in hot weather, but doesn't mind poor conditions and tolerates full sun and light shade. I grow mine in wooden boxes for winter salads. If you're starting it off in early autumn, cover it with fleece to get germination going, but once the seedlings are up they can withstand frosts. When sowing in the ground you can simply broadcast seed or plant out module-raised plants amongst tall growing vegetables. It will happily self-seed if left to its own devices.

BUNCHING ONIONS

Japanese bunching onions are a completely different matter from traditional onions. They're like huge spring onions, but better tasting, and the green part is just as good to cook as the white bulb. I sow throughout the growing season and overwinter some by sowing in late July or early August to grow big and fat over spring. They stand for longer than spring onions so you don't need to sow as often. I sow up to six seeds per module and plant them out 8cm (3in) apart. As you can eat them at any stage from 5cm (2in), I thin as I need to, allowing the last to grow big and fat. They are closely related to the Welsh onion and it is said that they can be left in place to become perennial, I haven't tried this yet though.

RADISHES

Radishes are easy to grow, and fast. They're a great tester to see if the soil has warmed up in spring, the minute radishes are up it's time to start sowing other things in earnest. Sow in drifts or lines and thin as necessary to about 5–10cm (2–4in) between plants. Pick as soon as the bulb appears on the surface as old radishes go hollow or woody in the middle. Spring radishes are the best, as they're tender and spicy, but not too hot with no over-powering aftertaste. Come midsummer they tend to run to seed without producing a nice round root, but they do produce tasty seed pods that are great stir-fried or as a lovely snack with beer. Young radish leaves are also good stir-fried or added to soups, so don't waste thinnings. The French trick of unsalted butter and fresh radish with a glass of white wine is lovely on an early summer evening.

There's a lot more to radishes than the traditional cherry red type with white tops. Summer radishes, or Oriental radishes such as mooli, produce giant white roots that can remain in the ground throughout a mild winter. 'Spanish Round' are black and fiery but perfect for Korean radish salads. Sow Oriental and summer radishes from July to August to harvest into the winter, they will need thinning to at least 15cm (6in) apart. A whole drift or line

This tomato was a beautiful 'Rose de Berne' heirloom that succumbed to blight, but at this point I was still dreaming of success.

of the same radish can be a bit boring so mix long and round varieties together. 'Cherry Belle' is cute as a button, round and red, and 'French Breakfast' is the standard, failsafe red and white radish. 'Black Spanish Round' is a hot winter radish that is dark black outside, white inside and very good cooked. 'April Cross' is a mooli radish with long white roots for autumn harvest. 'Minoawse' is also a pretty mooli variety.

FRUITING AND SEEDING VEGETABLES

TOMATOES

I have had my heart well and truly broken over tomatoes. It's not so much the fault of the tomatoes, but of blight, which seems so inevitable these summers. Growing outdoor tomatoes in our cool, wet climate is near on pointless. And yet I do. My approach is one that I hatched up with my father – invest nothing in your tomatoes other than fine soil. Don't pray, don't hope too much, don't even give your tomatoes more than a passing glance. Treat them as slightly awkward relatives that are a drag, but still need to be invited to the party. If you resign yourself to this there is a good chance that, even if blight comes, you'll get a tom or two (and preferably enough to bottle).

There are two types of tomatoes: indeterminate (cordons) and determinate (bush). Bush tomatoes are shorter and squatter than cordons and need very little attention. Cordon tomatoes grow as long as the season allows – you stop their growth by nipping out the growing tip to concentrate the growth to produce fruit, and you are also conventionally supposed to pinch out sideshoots and remove lower leaves. But while greenhouse or polytunnel growers would be wise to follow the rules, if you have only the space that nature gave you then treat the plant as nature would and leave it alone. This sort of no-intervention gardening has long been considered only for outcasts and cranks, but I'd like to see it brought to the heart of the mainstream. Tomatoes that are pinched out and nipped at are – in the big, bad world of blight – vulnerable. Every time you remove part of a plant, a healthy leaf or stem, you remove its ability to make its own energy so you weaken it a bit. This is the principle behind pruning, you remove part of a plant to make it grow more slowly, to grow in a certain direction or remove diseased or dying material. Pretty much anything you prune you shorten the life of (and to some extent weaken). We prune largely for aesthetics and because we've taken plants from their natural environment to grow them somewhere else, so we then have to prune to stop things growing too fast, or too leggy, and to force them to fruit or flower more. An unpruned apple tree lives far longer than a pruned one.

A tomato that has less green parts (and thus energy) has less of a chance to grow out of blight, which is possible (I've seen it with my own eyes). Also, every nipped out bit leaves a wound, a gaping hole that invites pests and diseases. I'm not alone, the Kokopelli Institute and The University of Davis, California, (among others) agree that pruning is akin to weakening the plant. The Kokopelli Institute allow their tomatoes to ramble about on the ground, others create teepees or ladders for the tomato to climb up. I have had mine supported in part by a rose bush. You do need to give the plants

Not my tomatoes, but Simon's (the photographer's) 'Gardeners' Delight'. He sent them to mock me when my harvest failed. He said that no one would know they weren't mine as they were scruffy looking with chamomile.

plenty of space, up to 1m (40in) between each, as they grow big and rather unruly. My one warning is that if you want large fruit under this regime you need to limit the plant to two fruit per vine. Pick off the excess fruit, but never the leaves.

Cultivating tomatoes

Wait until late March or April to germinate tomatoes indoors in gentle heat on a sunny windowsill or in a propagator. Tomatoes sown too early will grow leggy and take more time than our summers allow to get going. How many plants you need depends a little on how you like to gamble with blight, and how much space you can give them. I grew six last summer, four in the ground and two in tubs – all cordons. I germinated four seeds for each plant and chose the best ones. If your seedlings go leggy, plant them out with the stem buried up to the lower leaves as this will encourage the stem to turn to roots and help things along. This happens because there is a high level of a root-enabling hormone in the plant stem that only comes into play in the darkness where it commands the stems to produce roots.

The general spacing rule is to allow small bush tomatoes 50cm (20in) between each, and large cordons need at least 1m (40in). It's wise to plant companion plants with tomatoes, in a traditional vegetable garden this often means a welcome flurry of flowers, such as African marigolds that

have roots that release substances to ward off pests, or various basils or horehound that benefit tomato growth. For me, companion planting just means placing my tomatoes here and there in sun-baked spots along the back of the border, mingling them with the flowers.

Think of late summer colours when choosing flower combinations for toms. As most of the fruit will only really be visible when it ripens in late summer to early autumn, pair plants with similar slow-growing autumn flowers. Sunflowers are lovely behind tomatoes, or try shorter

More of Simon's mocking, but proof enough that tomatoes do grow well outside in the right sunny spots.

water one week and very little the next, especially as the fruit begins to swell. Over-watered plants will produce fruit that splits, under-watered plants will produce small fruit liable to fall off, and boom and bust watering will produce fruit with blossom end rot – inedible fruit with black bottoms. If you see flowers falling off without having the chance to set fruit this is usually because of extreme temperature fluctuation. Nights

Michaelmas daisies, chrysanthemums and other late daisy flowers, but do remember to leave plenty of space to get in and pick.

Tomatoes grown in pots need plenty of feeding, they are hungry crops. I feed mine every week with comfrey feed and add a good handful of chicken manure pellets to the pot before I plant them. Don't feed tomatoes growing in the ground as it is said that the best flavour comes from those grown with a little tough love. Watering in pots needs a little attention. Tomatoes may look very happy with over watering, but the fruits will taste watery. On hot days give the plants a long soak right through the pot, and make sure your watering is consistent, there is no point giving the plants lots of

below 13°C (55°F) or above 23°C (73°F) will cause flowers to fall.

The best varieties are those bred for your area. In the Midlands I have long favoured 'Kenilworth' or 'King George' because they were bred for market gardeners here and the tough skins mean they can take a summer of rain and then heat and then rain again. I look out for small, independent seed merchants who breed for the British climate, their experience is far more important that my desire to grow oddly named varieties. There's little wrong with first time growers sticking to the favourite 'Gardeners' Delight', which will produce good crops of well flavoured toms in even an average summer.

Chilli pepper (deceptively hot) and prolific. When tomatoes fail then a bounty of chillies in pots are a good condolence.

That said, there are lovely varieties to try, 'Brandywine' is huge, 'Millefleurs' produces hundreds of tiny toms, 'San Marzano' is great for pizzas and pasta. 'Legend' and 'Ferline' are early cropping F1 varieties that are supposed to have a degree of blight resistance. 'Aurora' is also worth trying on this count. However last year's summer was wet and dull, bringing epic amounts of blight and my every effort still resulted in brown plants. I only managed to harvest 23 green tomatoes that I ripened indoors.

Blight is brought on by airborne spores that overwinter in infected material. If you do get blight it is very important to either burn or bag infected material. Council compost is cooked to a temperature that will kill off any spores, but you should be scrupulous to remove any infected tomatoes or potatoes from your own. It is this infected material that allows the spores to persist in the ground until next year. But I'm still going to plant tomatoes next year, just in case ...

CHILLIES

If I could only grow one plant then it would always be chillies. It doesn't matter if you have sprawling acres, only a balcony or a windowsill, chillies are happy enough in just a pot. In the last few years chilli growing has gone from obscure to cult and there are now hundreds of varieties to choose from. Long, thin, fat, round, hot as hell or mild and sweet bright red, green, yellow, orange, purple and pink, large sprawling plants to

compact varieties perfect for a window ledge – there is a chilli for everyone.

I love the large and sprawling *Capsicum pubescens*, a short-lived perennial. I had the last plant for four years and have sent offspring around the world. It has lovely, slightly furry leaves and a very architectural habit, producing beautiful, cherry-red fruits that are just the right heat (though there is always one that blows your head off). I also grow a variety of purple and red ones as they look so pretty and some long, sweeter ones that can be stuffed.

Chillies are fairly easy to start from seed, as long as you get them going in good time to get enough growth to produce fruit. Sow around the beginning of March. They do need heat and can take a while to germinate, but they will get there, given a germination temperature of around 21°C (70°F), which is easiest if you have some sort of heat mat or propagator. Once the seedlings are up they need to move to slightly cooler conditions, around 18–20°C (64–68°F) to start conditioning them for our cooler climate.

Sow in seed trays and prick out at the three leaf stage, transplanting to small pots (a single sized yoghurt pot to start, and once they've grown a bit more, into a family sized yoghurt pot). Chillies like to be a little cramped, and they'll have to live indoors with you for at least a couple of months, only moving outside when any frost has passed and evenings are warm. Their ideal growing temperature is 18–21°C (65–70°F), they tend to turn sad and pale yellow if the temperature is any cooler.

You can plant them into the soil, in fact some of my tastiest chillies were grown outside. We sunk them in pots into the soil in a baked corner and got the hottest chillies in return. If you do plant them outside you'll need to lift them back into pots in autumn to take them inside, where the warmth of your house will often spur them on to produce more fruit, so you can pick well into winter.

The aim with chillies is good sturdy growth. Their natural pattern is to grow a single, straight stem that branches and, at the first branch, the king chilli is produced. This is a huge central chilli that tends to sap all the growth, so however pretty it looks, snap it off and eat it green. You'll get a lot more fruit as a result. Chillies need water and must never dry out, but prefer a good soaking once a week rather than dribs and drabs. Some books recommend feeding, but I think this spoils the flavour of the fruit, though a top-dressing of homemade compost or worm compost is a good addition.

TOMATILLOS

Tomatillo *Physalis ixocarpa* is a relative of the tomato, native to Mexico and a key ingredient in salsa verde. It is my summer saviour and the one tropical vegetable I always hold out for – when the tomatoes have gone down with blight and the sweetcorn has failed, my tomatillos always provide a crop.

The fruit is round, small and looks a lot like a miniature green tomato. It is covered by a papery husk called a calyx and when this bursts open, you know the fruit is ripe. It is possible to eat tomatillos raw, but I think they are at their best roasted with garlic and whizzed up into salsa or made into soups.

I find little to pick until September, though I imagine more southerly gardeners could pick much earlier. Sow indoors, as you would for tomatoes, in mid to late spring. You need more than one plant to pollinate so pot on several young seedlings into 9cm (3½in) pots and wait to plant them out until after the last frost. I have grown them happily in pots and in the ground, planting them about 30cm (12in) apart, so they are close enough to create a canopy that traps more heat in our cool climate. I also bury the stems up to the first leaves to promote more roots and bushy growth. Tomatillos are reasonably drought-tolerant, but will need regular watering if they are growing in pots. Prop up branches with twigs to avoid the fruit resting on the soil surface and being nibbled by slugs.

Mexican ground cherry *Physalis prunosa* is very closely related and grown in the same way. It's a slightly smaller plant, with smaller fruit and downy leaves, and is good for sprawling ground cover or in pots.

AMARANTH

There are two types of amaranth – grain and leaf. Grain amaranth requires a fair bit of space as it grows to 2m (6ft) and 50–60cm (20–24in) wide. It's arresting looking with great plumes of red flowers made up of thousands of seeds, but it does need hot summers to thrive. It is used widely in South America and Asian dishes (cook it much like quinoa, or couscous, for an excellent source of vitamin C, protein, iron and calcium), far outstripping tomatoes or spinach for nutritional value.

Leaf amaranth is easier for smaller spaces and a good substitute for spinach in hot summers. Red forms are ideal for weaving patterns in between vegetables. Green leaved forms (often known as calaloo or Indian spinach) are said to be the most productive. A very pale yellow form apparently tastes buttery – but I've yet to try it.

Amaranth needs soil about 20°C (68°F) to germinate so you can only sow it outdoors from June onwards, or sow in trays indoors and prick out into modules to be planted when space becomes available. Plants need a lot of water at the early stages, but once they get going they can tolerate periods of quite severe drought. Space plants about 8–10cm (3–4in) apart and harvest whole, young plants at about 20cm (8in) high. Or space them 20–25cm (8–10in) apart to pull individual leaves for continual harvesting through the summer.

'Red Army' is wildly decorative and looks lovely with pink and purple salvias. The seeds are tiny so don't sow too deeply, just gently press them into the soil. Allow any amaranth to go to seed with caution as they can get huge!

SWEETCORN

Sweetcorn is a useful vegetable to design with. It adds height, but in a delicate way so that it can be dotted through a bed, tiptoeing in and out of the spaces. It also provides a colourful show at the end of the summer, just as the garden is starting to look a little burnt out and the plants are coming to maturity and are all tassels and cobs. Sweetcorn is fickle about the weather and in a poor summer it won't do well, but it's worth a gamble for those fabulously sweet cobs.

You need to pick the right moment to germinate corn. It needs high temperatures to sprout, around 18°C (64°F), and warm soils to continue to grow. If the night-time temperature drops lower than 13°C (55°F), they sulk terribly. Sow from late May to mid June to have corn growing with the seasonal temperature, either sowing indoors to harden off or sow outside *in situ* from mid June, placing a jam jar over the seeds to trap in extra heat. The dried kernels are very hard and this tough seed will only soften in warm, wet conditions so the soil or compost needs to be well wetted and kept moist while the seeds are germinating. Pretty much all sweetcorn sown on the same day ripens on the same day so it's easy to get into a glut. Stagger your sowing dates for extended harvesting; plants grow very fast if conditions are right.

Sweetcorn needs around 45cm (18in) between each plant, though you can get away with slightly closer planting in rich and moisture-retentive soil. As plants are wind-pollinated they should be planted in blocks or circles, rather than scattered widely, or grow it in big pots and pollinate by hand. The male tassels appear at the top of the plant and the female silks below, you simply knock the plant to distribute pollen. Sweetcorn plants need moisture to produce good, fat cobs so mulch around young plants and interplant with other vegetables to create a living mulch – courgettes or pumpkins quickly cover the surface of the soil. Sweetcorn will not cope with competition at early stages, so you

Butternut squash 'Hunter' is bred for the British Isles and can be encouraged to clamber up sticks to reach the sun.

can't just squeeze it into spare spots around existing plants, I stick largely to drifts that suit its pollination pattern.

Corn is ready from late summer to mid autumn, but don't expect more than one or two cobs per plant, this is a treat not a subsistence course. The cobs are ready when the silks turn brown and the cobs are pale yellow, if they get too dark they are over-ripe. Press your thumbnail into a kernel, if the juice flows out clear it is still unripe, if it appears milky then it's ripe and if it doesn't have any juice it is over-ripe and best fed to the chickens.

There are many forms from sugary to super sweet, popcorn, minicorn and heritage bicolour varieties, which only do well in a tremendous summer. I recommend 'Tender Sweet', which are tender skinned, super sweet and slow to go starchy. Unless you're a stir-fry freak don't bother with minicorn.

COURGETTES, PUMPKIN AND SQUASHES

COURGETTES

Courgettes, marrows and summer squash are the same thing. Courgettes grow up to be marrows, and if you live outside the British Isles they're called summer squash. They are large plants that need at least 90cm (3ft) to bush out into, if spaced too close together they always get mildew as air can't circulate.

There is good reason to love the courgette. Pricey to buy, because they are fragile and difficult to transport without bruising or drying out, one healthy plant can produce as many as 25 courgettes in a single season. And they are truly handsome plants, large enough to command presence and with lovely, deeply cut, architectural leaves and brilliant yellow flowers that hold their own next to a fair few ornamentals.

Courgettes need to be sown with a little gentle heat, somewhere between 13–15°C (55–59°F) is ideal. Either sow indoors in late spring or (equally effective) outside under a jam jar in early spring. It's a myth that courgette seeds need to be sown pointed end down or else they rot off, you can sow them whichever way you like, just don't bury them more than 2–2.5cm (about 1in) deep. If you start them off inside you'll need to harden them off over at least two weeks, ideally in a coldframe or sturdy wooden box in the shelter of the house. Once prepared for outside life put them into good fertile soil with lots of extra homemade compost so they don't dry out. If you're putting them in the back or middle of a border try planting them on a slight mound as this raises the crown, making it easier to pick the fruit. If flowers or immature fruit fall off at the beginning of the season, this is because the flowers haven't been pollinated properly, you just have to wait for the plant to mature so that male and female flowers appear at the same time.

Courgettes grow into masses of space, which means a lot of bare ground at the beginning, so think about getting a crop of radishes or cut-and-come-again lettuce in before the courgettes take up the space. I like to sow a band of deep red

Above: It's a flying saucer! A yellow Patty Pan summer squash.
Opposite: The monstrous plant from which a bounty of flying saucers sprouted.

'Lollo Rosso' lettuce around the plant and pick it young. Surrounding the back of a yellow-fruiting courgette with some small sunflowers makes a picture-perfect autumn look. It's a good idea to plant courgettes and sweetcorn together, but I've never had much success using beans to climb up sweetcorn in the traditional 'Three Sisters' method. I find it makes it very hard to get in to pick the beans.

Keep an eye out for Patty Pan summer squash with their beautiful, big architectural leaves and bright, lemon-yellow flying saucers of fruit.

PUMPKINS AND WINTER SQUASHES

This covers a broad group of plants of varied shapes and sizes, from decorative snake gourds to fat orange pumpkins and blue-skinned squashes. If you have enough space do plant a few as they'll store for up to three months, and if you have more space than you need you can also plant them to make a very effective living mulch to do a little weed control on your behalf.

The medium sized trailing kabocha squash originates from Japan. With bluish–green skin and bright orange flesh, I think it has the finest flavour of all, but it does need a warm summer. 'Butternut' is the typical squash you see in supermarkets, shaped like a large ground nut with pale buff-coloured skin and light orange flesh. 'Sprinter' and 'Hunter' are good for cool summer climates. Hubbard types are sometimes known as acorn squash, but the group contains masses of different shapes, many with warty skin and colours ranging from blue to dark green and orange. 'Red Kuri' and 'Uchiki Kuri' are fine flavoured beasts, but do best in hot summers. 'Crown Prince' is good for cooler summers, a delicious hybrid with metallic blue skin and bright orange flesh. It has all the flavour of squash, but looks more like a pumpkin. Pumpkins are often bred for bravado and carving rather than eating. The flesh of the larger varieties is often rather watery and a bit tasteless, but 'Baby Bear' and other small types are good for soup and useful for their semi-huskless seeds that are tasty roasted.

Sow pumpkins and squashes as you would courgettes, though some need slightly higher temperatures. They're big sprawling crops that need space so don't go overboard, two or three are more than enough for most gardens. The planting hole should be roughly 30cm (12in) wide and deep, filled with well-rotted manure or compost (to act as a water-retentive reserve and food source to fuel that incredible growth) with a layer of soil on top. Spacing depends on the plants. Refer to the seed packet, but on the whole you need 1½m (5ft) between plants if they're going to trail on the ground, slightly less if you're encouraging them to climb up a structure. If you are going for climbers you can get a sowing of a quick-growing vegetable in at the same time before the climber shades out the ground below.

For pumpkins, put a stick at the base of the plant to show you where to water in dry months and then train the plant to circle round itself by gently pegging down the stem and circling round and round – I've found discarded tent pegs left at festivals ideal for the job. Once you have two or three immature fruit on a plant, 'stop' it by pinching out the tips and removing any surplus flowers or further fruit. This will concentrate growth into producing earlier and larger fruit, which is particularly important in a cooler summer. To get sun-ripened fruit you'll need to strip any shading leaves away towards the end of the season (say the beginning of September). It's also a good idea to raise fruit off the ground, an upturned plate is ideal, so that the undersides are exposed to the air. The longer you can leave the fruit on the plant the better they store, but they must be picked before the first frost.

To get the best flavour you need to cure the fruit when you pick them. Bring them into somewhere properly warm, ideally 24–27°C (75–81°F) and let them sit for a week to concentrate the sugars in the flesh. Then

God save our Gracious Queen, long live our noble cucumber sandwich.

they need to go into cold, but frost-free, airy storage around 7–10°C (45–50°F) where the skins will harden, and they should last well into winter.

CUCUMBER

Outdoor cucumbers aren't that attractive, the yellow flowers are jolly, but not a patch on courgettes, and the tough-looking leaves aren't great, but they will give you cucumber sandwiches, pretty much whatever the weather. I think they've slightly fallen by the wayside because of their tough, sometimes prickly, skins, but the flesh tastes so good, and nothing could be simpler to grow.

Choose the right type

Indoor cucumbers are the type you find in the supermarket, thin-skinned, sensitive sorts that need molly-coddling. Outdoor, thick-skinned toughies don't mind the odd drop in temperature and once they get going they laugh in the face of pests and diseases. These are sometimes referred to as ridge cucumbers as they were traditionally grown on small ridges to improve drainage. They are more sprawlers than climbers and well-suited to container growing. Heirlooms look slightly more refined, often palest yellow or green and shaped more like lemons and apples than

cucumbers. Some are delicious and some are just curious. Peel the skins of prickly forms to get at the delicious flesh beneath. Yellow heirloom 'Crystal Apple' is crisply delicious. 'Marketmoor' has good mildew resistance and old school fruit. 'Kyoto' produces long, thin Japanese types that are particularly good for cooking – I believe cucumber soup is a wonderful thing.

Gherkins are stubbly little fruits rarely more that 5cm (2in) long. They're good for pickling, particularly with lots of dill, but equally good raw. Hybrid outdoor forms, 'American Burpless' or Japanese varieties, are thinner-skinned, long-fruited but tough enough for very productive outdoor cultivation. They need space as they can grow up to 1½m (about 5ft) tall, and anything I may say about a cucumber not being attractive is forgiven when you have a plant dripping in fruit.

How to make a cucumber happy

Cucumbers are easy enough from seed. They need a little heat to germinate, around 20°C (68°F), and hate to be transplanted so you need to sow them in a pot at least 9cm (3½in) deep. Don't sow before mid spring and don't overwater as young seedlings easily succumb to damping off. Once your plants have two or three true leaves and look sturdy you can harden them off, but don't put them out if there's any danger of the temperature dropping below 10°C (50°F) or they will sulk and become very susceptible to slug attacks.

Choose a sunny spot with good fertile soil to which you've added extra compost. The base of the stem can rot off fairly easily so make sure it sits above soil level – growing on a mound or ridge can help to keep excess water away from the base. Plant climbers 45cm (18in) apart and sprawlers around 90cm (3ft) apart. To make the best use of space, train them up trellises, mesh supports or around teepees of canes, you may need to tie them in at the early stages, but they'll soon make their own way. Mine grow against a warm, southwest-facing brick wall. In the early stages I lean an old window against the wall to trap that extra bit of heat.

Right: Cucumber 'Marketmoor' is prolific and tasty. The top is classic slug damage, but it doesn't affect the flesh.

Overleaf: Apple 'Discovery' is a sweet, very early apple that is ready for September. Behind nestles a large rhubarb and some raspberries. In the foreground is Liatris spicata, a long-lasting cut flower (and beloved by bees).

Be vigilant about slugs and do whatever you can to control them, as they are a real problem with young plants. If roots appear on the surface of the soil (as they often do), cover them with compost or mulch to conserve water. Mosaic virus is transmitted by aphids and generally appears in midsummer, when the plants are just getting going, causing mottled and distorted leaves. Powdery mildew causes white patches on the leaves. You can control both to some extent by spraying with a solution of equal parts milk and water.

DESIGN TIPS

Train cucumbers to hide walls and fences or up teepees to add height to a bed. They grow well in pots and containers as long as you provide support. Once they are up and growing it's a good idea to grow something around their base to shade the roots and conserve moisture. I've had good success with red clover, wild strawberries, violas and marigolds (*Calendula officinalis*).

THE FOREST GARDEN

Forest gardening was pioneered by Robert Hart in the 70s, though recently Patrick Whitefield has written *How to Make a Forest Garden* that has done much to popularize this form of gardening.

When forest gardens work they can be low maintenance, highly productive gardens, but you do end up eating very odd things. Lime leaves are your salads, nuts are your nibbles and it's best if you like lemon balm a lot. It's a radical departure for our diet, but offers a way of creating ecologically diverse, useful and habitat-rich back gardens.

Forest gardens work on the principle that they mimic the woodland edge so you have tall trees, a middle storey of shrubs and then ground cover, but instead of woodland plants you use fruiting trees, perennial vegetables and herbs. A typical structure would be to have a fruit tree, under it a soft fruit bush and then a groundcover herb, such as lemon balm or wild strawberries. In a forest garden every plant has a purpose, mostly for eating. You don't do any digging and you run the garden like a forest, allowing leaf litter to build up and recycling nutrients back into the soil. You also mulch with comfrey and other nutrition-rich plants, and harvest little and often.

I have a bastardized version by the chicken coup where I grow apples, raspberries, rhubarb, wild and cultivated strawberries, currants, lemon balm and granny's bonnets (because they look so pretty amongst the strawberries, but then that's where I fail as a forest gardener – I like pretty, useless things).

Don't try and grow more than four plants if there are just two of you, as the more you harvest the more you eat. Try to pick them small and tender, if you do allow them to grow supermarket long, cut the bottom half off to eat and leave the rest attached. This will callous over and you can pick it later.

HERE TO STAY: PERENNIAL VEGETABLES

Perennial vegetables, such as rhubarb and asparagus, are having a bit of renaissance, thanks to the 'Slow Food' movement, the general desire to eat locally grown food and a growing interest in forest gardening. All of a sudden, old-school vegetables like perennial nine star broccoli are appearing back in seed catalogues and gardens, though I'm still hunting for a source of the lost 'Daubenton' perennial kale that forms huge plants with masses of young shoots in spring. For the busy urban gardener perennial vegetables offer a perfect solution – something to eat with little effort other than establishing them.

Once perennial plants are established, there they will stay, so it pays to make sure they go into a good home. Plant them into a generous sized hole, backfilled with good, rich compost and mulch to double your luck. To get decent crops, you should mulch at least once a year in autumn or spring with something rich and nutritious, such as well-rotted manure or homemade compost. It pays to weed well, as many perennial vegetables hate to have their roots disturbed and if you don't get out the peskier weeds at the beginning, you will regret it later – I say this from experience. Also, make sure you clear up any diseased leaves in autumn to prevent problems building up.

Don't harvest rhubarb or globe artichokes the first year, and you need to leave asparagus for two years. Allow the roots to bed down and become truly established before you start demanding a crop back every year.

ARTICHOKES
The two main different types of artichoke have nothing in common. Globe artichokes are the most worthwhile. Handsome and hugely expensive from the shops, once established these stunning vegetables are incredibly easy to grow. Tuberous Jerusalem artichokes split the world firmly into two camps, you can either digest them or you can't and if you can't you will fart a lot, hence their nickname fartichokes.

I love Jerusalem artichokes, my mother makes a fine soufflé out of them and they screen out unsightly views. The plants grow very tall, up to 3m (10ft). They are hardy, tough and happy in a neglected, shady corner, but as they are as handsome as very

Globe artichoke 'Green Globe' (both here and previous page) is a very prolific grower that provides plenty of large heads to eat once established.

tall sunflowers they shouldn't necessarily be relegated to a forgotten place.

Some people find Jerusalem artichokes invasive and to this I can only say they don't eat them enough. I note every new plant with pleasure, dig them up each autumn (thoroughly at that) and then chuck an egg sized one back for next year. I think part of the problem is that it is traditional to leave them in the ground over winter and once they've been cut back they can be hard to find. If they do start to appear in spring, dig them up with the first sign of growth. Or you can grow them in big pots, around the size of a half barrel.

Plant out tubers in late winter or early spring, roughly 30cm (12in) apart and about 10cm (4in) deep, although they will cluster up much closer once established. Harvest from late October onwards, after cutting down the towering stems, if the ground isn't too wet you can leave them in the ground all winter, but mark the soil with cut stems so you know where to dig. Leave one or two large tubers behind for next year's crop. They are very knobbly so a bit of a fiddle to prepare, but after a good scrub they can be boiled, stir-fried, roasted or baked in a gratin (my favourite way). Cooking them with winter savory seems to reduce their gassy properties.

Globe artichoke is my desert island vegetable, the one that I would rush to the sea to save, my finest, favourite flavour. (My editor has pointed out that I have two favourite plants, chillies and artichokes,

the chillies are being washed out to sea as I write.) I grow the USA bred 'Green Globe', with fat green heads, and the delicate purple 'Violetta di Chioggia', which is much smaller, but by far the prettiest vegetable in my garden. With their beautiful, serrated, silvery leaves most are ridiculously pretty, and they're quite common in herbaceous borders. They require good fertile soil, sun and a little shelter, being happiest against a warm wall or in a sun-drenched spot. There is no point growing a measly looking one, so do give them the conditions they like.

You can start them by purchasing young plants, grow from seed or from an offshoot of a mature plant. With all methods you will have to wait before you can eat any delicious leafy heads. The plants have to be big before you start cutting. Plant 90cm (3ft) apart, and plant low-growers between them to fill up the gaps while the artichoke gets established. I have thyme and pink-flowering strawberries around the base of mine. If you've taken an offshoot you should plant it deeper than the previous position, as they have a tendency to uproot themselves. Watch out for drying winds or long periods without rain as they can easily dry out. Seed-raised plants can vary a great deal in looks, so sow the whole packet (you won't get many seeds) and in the second season weed out any less than pretty ones.

Cut off the first head when it is fairly small, this will send the plant into a frenzy of production. You should get at least four or five good sized heads from a mature plant, as they grow older and develop into a clump, expect to get more. You can eat almost all of the head if you pick it young, discarding the furry centre of stamens. Artichokes are best steamed or lightly boiled and then you can eat each leaf dripping in French vinaigrette or melted butter.

The plants aren't keen on very low temperatures or prolonged, wet winters so cover them with fleece or straw to protect them over winter, and keep checking for slugs as they emerge in spring.

ASPARAGUS

The house where I grew up had asparagus beds of such calibre that we all grew sick of eating the spears. As a child nothing seemed to slow the prodigious output of these beds. It's only as an adult that I realise my mother's hard work and constant weeding were actually the source of the bounty. The first meal of asparagus marked the beginning of summer. It was always eaten outside, the fat spears dripping in butter. We were so decadent that we merely ate the head and gave the rest to the chickens. Until my parents moved, I received several very heavy parcels every summer of my mother's asparagus, often with her eggs too. Asparagus spears dipped in a soft boiled egg is still my favourite comfort food.

This year I planted my first asparagus. Not the wide mounded bed they are traditionally grown on, as that would take up the best part of my garden, but in little clusters along with *Eremurus* flowers (tall, fluffy, yellow flowers like foxtails) in a spare patch by the fence. Basically I've substituted asparagus for tall ornamental grasses in my garden. Where I used *Stipa* or *Calamagrostis* to create a light, waving pattern, I'm now using asparagus and it seems a very satisfactory swap. Asparagus takes a long time to settle, it's three years before you can pick the spears and in that time it is important that they

are not out-competed or out-shadowed by other plants. You can only raise fast, low-growing crops, such as radish or cut-and-come-again lettuce, between establishing asparagus plants.

When you plant asparagus spread out their roots so they look like spider's legs on each side of a small mound, and then cover them with good compost. Initially these roots may become exposed, so just keep covering them up.

GARLIC CHIVES

Chinese or garlic chives are an excellent garlic substitute for the patio grower. They are pretty to look at with delicate, starry white flowers that are very good for cutting for a vase, and flat, bright-green leaves. They are unfussy about conditions, but prefer good, fertile soil and a pot at least 20cm (8in) deep. They are fairly slow to clump up, so you shouldn't crop them the first year. Find some from other gardeners if you can, though I have successfully sown from seed in the spring and planted

out decent pot-grown plants the following spring. Increase your stock by dividing established clumps in spring or autumn. I have them running along the edge of my path between parsley and ordinary chives. In very warm summers they set seed, so pinch off the flowers if you don't want them crossing with normal chives.

They are happy in full sun, but if the soil is too dry they produce very tough stems that are little use for cooking. They do best in my garden where they are slightly shaded by other, taller plants.

HORSERADISH

I have lovely childhood memories of harvesting wild horseradish on Sunday mornings in autumn for lunch. The thick leaves smell strongly of horseradish, but you had to hunt around to find decent roots, though you don't need much to make a killer sauce. Horseradish is found in damp places, marshy spaces and by streams. There are great swathes along my local path that runs along the river but as it isn't legal to dig

Rhubarb is an excellent source of Vitamin C at a point when there is little fruit in the garden. The other bonus is that you have to do very little to make a rhubarb happy.

your own from public places, you may need to grow it. It is a big plant and wants to be highly invasive so it's best grown in a large pot. Don't overfeed your plants or you'll get all leaf and little root, and although they're pretty adaptable they do prefer it moist.

You'll need two growing seasons before you can harvest decent sized roots about 2.5cm (1in) in diameter. The best time to harvest is autumn when the leaves have died back after a summer of growth, but you can harvest roots from a healthy plant at pretty much any time, see it as thinning the plant. Only harvest what you need as the roots don't store well.

PERENNIAL BROCCOLI
Perennial broccoli is actually a cauliflower masquerading as broccoli. It's a terrifically old-fashioned cottage garden vegetable. Each spring it produces a small, central cauliflower, cut this off and it sends the plant into production of many broccoli-like side shoots. The only known variety is called 'Perennial Nine Star Broccoli', the 'nine stars' referring to the masses of broccoli-like stems.

Sow in spring in modules and plant out in a carefully chosen space, once frost has passed, spacing the plants 90cm (3ft) apart. Expect the first spears the following spring. It grows best in sheltered areas or may need staking elsewhere, and as it can go on producing for five years, site it well. Pigeons love it, so net the plants if necessary.

Cut the main head off first and then eat subsequent shoots and leaves. By late spring the plant will stop producing side shoots and run to seed, at this point cut back all remaining shoots. Expect to replace plants every four years or so on a rota so that you have several in production and young ones coming up behind.

PERENNIAL ONIONS
The Welsh onion, or Japanese leek, is an old cottage garden favourite, providing white stems and fleshy leaves to eat whatever the weather. You harvest as you would a giant spring onion, chopping it off at soil level. The green leaves are chive-like, quite mild and good chopped up in salads or stir-fried. The stems are like large, strong spring onions, and good sautéed like a traditional onion or steamed with rice. The easiest way to get these going is to find someone with an existing clump as they need to be divided fairly regularly and there are always some spares. Otherwise it is reasonably easy to sow seeds in situ, thinning to 10–15cm (4–6in) apart and allowing plants to bulk up in clusters. By its second season large, creamy-white flowers should appear, resembling large chive flowers and can be used the same way, as an excellent winter menu addition.

The rarer ever-ready or everlasting onion *Allium cepa* var. *perutile* is similar to the Welsh onion but with flatter leaves. It's more of a curiosity than a must-have.

Egyptian walking onion, or tree onion, is a perverse creature. If it takes to you, you're overrun with it, and if it doesn't, you lust after it. It's a bulb onion with a cluster of baby onions growing out of the stem tip. The stems eventually bend under the weight of

these baby onions and once they touch the ground they tumble off to set root, or walk around your garden. The little bulbils are too fiddly to peel, so harvest like a Welsh onion by cutting stems at the base, leaving several plants untouched to reproduce. Tree onions can reach 1m (40in), and are interesting looking plants that throw out great shapes when left to their own devices.

RHUBARB

Rhubarb is the best known perennial vegetable, every garden should have at least one plant. It fills that hungry, late spring gap and, despite being known mainly as a pudding ingredient, it is excellent with oily fish or chicken. It's a fine looking plant, large leaved and graceful with the sort of

Previous spread: Majestic purple sprouting broccoli.
Opposite: Ice plant nestles among Golden oregano, chives and, to the left, buckwheat grown as a green manure, but left to flower for the bees.

architectural presence that garden designers should go wild for, but it's been largely ignored because it's edible. Now is the time to up its profile and it is one plant you really should add to your garden. It's a doddle to grow, shade-tolerant, pest and disease free and heavenly when cooked well.

Rhubarb has deep roots that dive down into the soil, so leave it be in the first year because if you disrupt the roots you've had it. Once it's got going little will stop it. It will survive in very poor soils, but does best in nitrogen-rich soils that are moisture-retentive, but have good drainage – if it sits in a puddle all winter long it will rot off. A thick layer of rich, organic mulch every spring will help the plant along no end. You can pick from late spring to early summer. Most plants become increasingly acidic as summer continues, though some modern varieties keep their sweetness. You can force rhubarb to produce from February onwards by keeping the plant in the dark with either a large bucket or a forcing pot placed over it in January to get tall, pale, tender stems. Slugs love these tender stems, so you need to be vigilant about picking them off on a daily basis.

Divide your plants roughly every 10 years in early autumn, discarding any dried or shrivelled bits and replanting sections in compost-rich soil. By then, the middles will have become woody and centre stalks may flower regularly – you need to remove spikes to keep leaf production going. By dividing

WHICH TO CHOOSE?

IF YOU HAD TO GROW JUST ONE:
Rhubarb. It pays back the most, it is easy to establish, does well in partial shade, fills the hungry gap in spring and is a rich source of vitamin C.

IF YOU HAD SPACE FOR TWO:
Asparagus, although a little tricky to set up, is the most financially rewarding crop.

IF YOU'RE STUCK WITH SHADE:
Mitsuba is a wonderful herb to add to salads, soups and as a garnish. It's as pretty as a picture and the red version is happiest in shade, so it's useful for those awkward spaces.

the plant and keeping the outer buds you renew energy and growth.

Of my four plants, two grow by established apple trees, basking in their dappled shade, but don't grow rhubarb by young trees as their deep roots can compete. Clumps of pale green stemmed 'Timperley Early' nestle among ferns and grasses by the apple, pretty blush-pink 'Champagne' has a back of border position where it can be admired with perennial sweet peas twirling through it, and classic red 'Victoria' sat last year among chicory flowers and broad beans, which were picked before the rhubarb dominated the space.

OTHER CURIOSITIES

Myoga, or Japanese ginger, is a relatively hardy ginger grown for its young shoots and stems. It's one of those plants that gets hardier as it becomes more established. It can spread rather vigorously if it finds the right semi-shady conditions. You eat the young, unopened flowers and leaves, never the rhizome.

Mitsuba, or Japanese parsley, is a common herb in Japan and little seen elsewhere. It tastes like a mix of parsley, celery and angelica. I grow mine as a curious perennial, cutting it down several times a season to re-sprout and I use it as a parsley substitute. It's main advantage is that it likes to grow in shade, making it a useful and attractive plant for places where few edible plants will grow.

HERBS

If I had only a window ledge to grow on I would fill it with herbs. They make frozen dinners into something special, they take a pasta sauce from boring to brilliant in

HERBS TO GROW FROM SEED

Basil and chives do best sown with a little heat in a propagator or on a warm windowsill. Sow them in spring and plant out after the last frost. Basil is sent to a mushy grave by the first frost, so pick all you can before autumn and process it.

Parsley is very slow to germinate, so be patient. Sow in late July or mid August, when day temperatures are warm enough to speed germination. Curly parsley is more hardy than Italian flat, but both will go through snow if they are covered with a cloche.

Coriander can be sown from late spring to early autumn (it will overwinter under a cloche). It will run to seed in hot weather, so sow in batches for successional pickings. Leaf coriander is least likely to bolt, while lemon coriander is very tender and should be sown in late spring for summer pickings.

French Sorrel is a herb that provides leaves for much of the year.

seconds, they define an omelette, and then there are the glories of herb teas. Herbs are generally small plants that are packed with flavour, the essential oils in their leaves releasing great bursts of scent and taste. The problem with many shop-bought ones is that they are grown soft and lush in polytunnels and don't have the flavour of their outside cousins. An outdoor basil rarely looks like the stuff in supermarkets, it has tougher leaves, it's a bit nibbled here and there, it has war wounds and scars – but it tastes all the better because of it.

Homegrown herbs have life experience, and that makes them much better tasting. I grow many herbs in pots as the more

HERBS TO BUY AS PLANTS

If you buy your herbs as plants (bay or tarragon, for example, would take several years to make a half decent sized plant from seed), try to buy them in late spring to give them a summer of growing before life gets difficult.

Rosemary. The prostrate form is low-growing, ideal for windowboxes.

Lavender. *Lavandula angustifolia* 'Nana Alba', a white-flowering dwarf variety that is good for windowboxes.

Sage. *Salvia officinalis* 'Tricolor' is splashed purple, green and white and can be kept compact by regular pruning.

Feverfew. This can be bought as either seeds or plant, but it's easiest just to buy a plant and let it seed itself.

Thyme.

Winter savory.

Oregano/marjoram. *Origanum vulgarum* 'Compactum' is ideal for pots.

Mints.

Bay.

tender herbs are easy to look after this way. Tarragon, various sages, lemon verbena and lavenders are rarely killed by the cold in my garden, but have been drowned in the wet. Even when I plant them in almost pure grit, my underlying bed of clay soaks them to within an inch of their lives, whereas in a pot I can control their environment. Those that don't like too much water get moved to a sheltered spot, those that need heat come indoors to the kitchen, and those that are just too rumbunctious (the mints) are confined by their pots.

Rosemary, thyme, lavender, winter savory and oregano are all herbs from the Mediterranean, so for the best flavours grow them a little tough and make sure they never spend the winter sitting in wet soils. They thrive in poor, free-draining soil and can be kept bushy by regular harvesting. I chop my thymes back in June to get a second flush of leaves later on. I leave oregano to flower as the bees love it and it responds well to an autumn cutback, sitting as a low mound of leaves over winter.

WINDOWSILL HERBS
You can grow a variety of herbs on the kitchen windowsill, but herbs require high light levels so even the sunniest window will not offer enough for a

long life indoors. Expect to replace indoor herbs up to three times a year. You can grow some lusher herbs as microgreens (sown and then cut at seedling stage somewhere between 8–10cm (20–25in) tall). Grow these in takeaway trays or 9cm (3½in) pots. Lovage, dill, coriander, rocket and fennel pack a punch even at such a tender age. Something like dill will take ten days to be up and ready to use. Sow fairly thickly as you are just harvesting tiny leaves. Choosing to grow herbs this way will mean resowing seedlings every month or so, but you can still be picking fresh dill in winter.

Basil microgreens growing on a window to be cut when very small and tasty.

LESS USUAL HERBS

I would find it hard to live without herbs. Some I use for teas, some I use infrequently, but only want to use fresh, some I guess I just collect. Mints are my weakness, I have too many that are just oh so slightly different. Even if you only use these herbs once a season they are attractive enough to claim a space in your garden.

Tender Vietnamese coriander, *Polygonum odoratum* has a distinct flavour somewhere between lemon and coriander. It has red stems and green leaves with red chevrons marking each leaf. I grow mine in a pot in a sunny spot, but the red chevrons do fade in strong sun. In South East Asia it is added to meat and egg dishes, just a few leaves will fragrance an entire dish. I also add it to stir-fries where I might use coriander. It has to be brought inside for winter.

Cuban oregano, *Plectranthus amboinicus* is a strongly oregano/sage-flavoured herb that works very well with meat and fish dishes and can be used with beans and salads. It's extremely tender so can only really be grown in a pot that must be brought inside for the winter, where it makes a great house plant with thick, fleshy leaves rather like *Coleus*. Although it hails from South East Asia it's used mainly in Cuban, Mexican and Jamaican foods. Propagate from stem cuttings in summer and pinch out straggly growth to keep the plant bushy. Pick little and often all year round.

Sorrel, *Rumex acetosa* is a perennial herb with tart, lemon-flavoured leaves and attractive pale-green young leaves. It thrives in damp soil in partial shade or sun.

I have a clump that is happily established in an old winebox. Sow seeds in spring and thin to 20cm (8in) between plants. Flavour begins to deteriorate once the plant has flowers, so chop off flowering stems and divide plants to keep them vigorous. Young sorrel leaves are very good sparingly used in salads and in egg dishes, or with soft cheese. Buckler-leaf sorrel, *Rumex scutatus*, is perhaps more attractive with its spear shaped leaves. Bloody sorrel, or bloody dock, *Rumex sanguineus* is the prettiest of the bunch with deep blood-red veins and midribs, but it is extremely tart and only the youngest leaves are edible. I like to edge paths with it.

Perilla (also known as Shiso), *Perilla frutescens* 'Crispa' is used mainly in Japanese cuisine. I grow the beautiful dark red form. Green and purple forms are used to flavour raw fish, bean curd, tempura and pickles. The purple form is used to colour pickles, fish and ume plums. It has a slightly sweet metallic taste that takes a little getting used to. I use mine in omelette, the very young top leaves in salads and a lot in pickles. It's a half-hardy annual, sown from seed in spring into well-drained soil in partial shade or sun and spaced 20cm (8in) apart. You may be able to buy it as a bedding plant. Use leaves throughout the summer, stems can also be cooked and the seeds are edible too.

Perennial Sweet Cicely, *Myrrhis odorata* contains a volatile oil that tastes and smells strongly of anise. It is sweet, exceptionally good with rhubarb and other stewed fruit and lovely in yoghurt. The young leaves are good in salads, but best of all it's very beautiful. It has fine, fern-like foliage and

Opposite: Sweet cicely and curly kale blend so well that they confuse the cabbage white butterflies and pigeons who can't find the kale they so like to eat.
Right: Outdoor basil has tougher leaves but more flavour for cooking.

pretty white flowers, and is happiest in partial shade in rich soil. It can seed itself around a bit, but can also be very slow to germinate so try to find someone with a clump and take a well-rooted division in spring. It dies back in winter, but you can freeze fresh leaves for winter use.

OTHER PRETTY HERBS

Basils like it warm and sulk in cold summers. It's worth taking the gamble though, not just for their fine flavour, but because so many are highly ornamental. Sow in spring and pinch out the growing tips to encourage bushiness and delay flowering. Plant out when all signs of frost have passed, between 10–25cm (4–10in) apart depending on the variety. Use the purple ones to edge beds or to contrast with green lettuces. Look out for very purple and ruffled 'Purple Ruffles', and 'Red Rubin'. The very large leaved 'Neapolitanum' is a showstopper, but it hates being cold and slugs seem to love this one even more than they love the others – and they do. It's one for a baking patio.

Compact basils for pots and windowsills
'Compact' and 'Dwarf' are perfect for pots and Greek basils have tiny, very potent leaves that seem to resist slug damage better than others. Aniseed and Thai basils always want to flower, so let them as they're very pretty.

ORNAMENTAL FRUIT

Ripening apples, fragrant strawberries, jars of raspberry jam, the first blueberries on a bowl of cornflakes – I get these and much more from my small garden, with very little effort on my part. A productive garden without some fruit would truly be a sin.

Traditionally, fruit in walled gardens is trained along the protective walls in complicated fans and espaliers away from winds and frosts. Many urban gardens have similar set ups, not perhaps beautiful bricks walls, but wooden fences and other buildings make just as suitable spots for training fruit. A sunny, south-facing wall could accommodate figs, peaches or nectarines. A vine could be grown to create privacy from neighbours and offer seasonal interest, as well as fruit. In small spaces standard gooseberries or

cordon currants can be tucked into corners or grown in pots.

Once established, fruit trees do not need much work, other than pruning out crossing, diseased or damaged branches in winter. Espalier, cordon and other trained trees need pruning to promote spur growth (where next years fruit will appear), but this is simple to do once you've been shown how. For a focal point in a garden I don't think you can go wrong with a quince tree, majestic-looking with large leaves, creamy-white flowers and, in autumn, beautiful yellow fruit with their own distinct fragrance. The small weeping mulberry with gnarled branches, *Morus alba* 'Pendula', is another glorious fruit tree. Both will be productive within five years of planting a two-year-old tree. Many highly ornamental crab apples are grafted onto dwarfing rootstocks to produce small, prolific trees that offer spring flowers and autumn colour and fruit. 'John Downie' is a larger form, covered with yellow fruit that is considered to be the best for jam and jelly. *Malus* x *zumi* 'Golden Hornet' is a small tree festooned with bright yellow fruit and a mass of flowers in spring, *Malus* x *robusta* 'Red Sentinel' has cherry-red fruit that hang on the tree for a long time, right through autumn until Christmas, and *Malus hupehensis* has lovely pink blossom and rosy fruit.

For an informal look, berries such as blackberries, hybrid berries and kiwis can be trained up pergolas or along arches. Where you are restricted to containers you can still grow figs, blueberries, genetically dwarfed nectarines, such as 'Nectarella' and 'Garden Lady', peaches, apples and pears on very dwarfing rootstocks, pomegranates, vines – all are possible in 25 litre or larger pots. The trees can be underplanted with

ROOTSTOCKS

● Apples are sold on a variety of different rootstocks, which determine how large a tree will grow.

● For small gardens M27 very dwarfing stock is best for fertile soils. This produces the smallest trees that grow 1.5–2m (5–6ft) tall. Trees suitable for containers are generally grown on this stock.

● M26 dwarfing stock is best for ordinary soils. Trees will grow 2–3m (6–10ft) high.

● M9 very dwarfing stock trees will also grow to 2–3m (6–10ft).

● Other rootstocks are only really suitable for larger gardens, though you may get away with MM106 semi-dwarfing stock that allows trees to reach 4–6m (13–20ft).

● For pears, look for those grafted onto Quince C stock.

● Plums aren't available on very dwarfing rootstocks, but can be trained into fan shapes or pyramids for a more economic use of space.

Raspberry 'Autumn Bliss' was so prolific that it produced fruit from September to November.

strawberries in early spring and you could be picking fruit by summer. Tender fruit, such as citrus or olives (you'll be hard pressed to get a crop of olives, but the leaves are very good in tea when you have a cold), can be grown in pots and moved into sheltered areas for the winter.

If you want to train fruit as espaliers or fans against a wall or along a boundary it's best to get an expert to help start you off, but it's an even better plan, and quite affordable, to buy a two- or three-year-old, pre-trained tree. You can either start with bare-root trees (sold between November and March) or buy container-grown specimens. Your first task is to establish strong, galvanized, horizontal steel wires to tie the tree to. The wires need to be taut, and at least 5cm (2in) away from walls to allow air to circulate. Attach wires to your wall or fence, or firmly installed posts, with vine eyes, roughly 20cm (8in) apart, with the lowest about 40cm (15in) off the ground. These horizontal wires will give you a framework for your tree. The way your wall or fence faces will determine what you can grow against it. South-facing walls will accommodate tender fruit, such as nectarines and peaches, but apples, plums, grapes and pears will be equally as happy on a south or west-facing wall. You'll have to make sure that the soil retains moisture so as not to bake the fruit.

With good soil at the base of north-facing walls you can grow blackberries, cordon gooseberries, morello cherries and redcurrants. East-facing walls get more morning light so you can get away with anything that grows on a north wall plus apples, pears and, if sheltered enough, plums. If you are in a frost-prone area choose late-flowering varieties, but check which do well locally.

Once the basic framework has been established in winter, trained trees are pruned in summer for the first year or two after planting to keep productive and in shape. The smallest fruit trees are step-over cordons, very small trees bent over to create a low-growing living fence which can be very productive and often used to line a path, but you can't forget to prune them. Take advice from specialist fruit growers as to what will grow where, what sort of support to use. Apple trees are not self-fertile so you need two or more to pollinate the flowers. In suburban areas there is usually one fairly near in the neighbourhood, but in inner cities this

can be more of an issue, especially as you need two varieties that flower at the same time. For the most popular choices this won't be a problem, but if you are choosing something rarer you need to find out what time it blooms.

It's almost impossible to recommend varieties of apples, there are so many and preference is particularly individual. Apple Day is held on the 21st of October every year and there are celebrations across the country. It's a chance to take unidentified apples to experts, eat a wide variety of apples, drink cider and juice and meet nurseries who grow and sell heritage fruit. If you want to find something special, local to where you live, something that will fruit at a specific time or store well, then go to an Apple Day, eat loads of fruit and make your choice.

My favourite apples include 'Blenheim Orange' (good storer and perfumed flavour),

HOW TO PLANT A FRUIT TREE

The cheapest apple trees are sold as bare-root trees, from late autumn to early spring when the tree is dormant and can be lifted without disturbing the roots. They must be planted soon after arriving to avoid drying out, if there's a delay keep them wrapped up somewhere cool, dark and frost-free until you can plant; or heel them into a spare patch of ground. They are best planted on a slight mound (imagine a saucer turned upside down, but the top of the mound needs to be lower than the soil level). Stick the centre of the tree on the mound, spread the roots around evenly and then cover with soil and mulch. The mulch will conserve water and keep down weeds. You will need to tie the tree to an upright stake, as you do not want the tree to rock and snap the graft. If rabbits are about, put a guard around the base as rabbits love the bark.

Even if you plant container-grown trees or bushes it's still best to plant in autumn or winter or you'll have to be extra careful about keeping the tree well watered. A tree or bush that doesn't get enough water in its first year will die. Before you plant, fill the planting hole up with water and let it drain away, then the soil around the plant will already be saturated when you first water the tree so more water will be available for the new roots, rather than instantly draining away. The hole should be twice the width of the pot that tree came in. Gently tease the roots out, make a little mound to spread them across and backfill it with soil – don't fill with compost or the roots won't bother to explore the soil around them.

You will need to water a tree in well for a month after planting and then throughout the season if the weather is dry for more than two weeks. Give it a good soak, at least two or three cans of water per tree. Trees on the most dwarfing stock, M27 and M9 will also need constant staking.

'Winter Banana' (rosy yellow and tastes like it's name suggests), 'Tydeman's Late Orange' (a stronger 'Cox's Orange' good for storing) and 'Egremont Russet' (a fine, fine apple).

I'll eat any pear going, 'Concord' and 'Beth' are both quick to crop with excellent flavour. 'Doyenne du Comice' is a tasty heritage variety, but it does need a sunny spot to do well in.

'Vranja' is one of the most popular quinces, with a lovely scent to the fruit. They flower very early so need to be sited somewhere sheltered and you must make sure they're not in a frost pocket.

FIGS

In a sheltered spot, on a sun-drenched patio or a south-west facing wall, you can grow magnificent, fat, juicy figs. This doesn't happen every year, as our climate is too fickle, but in the sunny years that you do get fruit the memory is almost good enough to make up for the years that you don't. For good crops you must restrict the tree's growth; grow a fig in a pot – line the planting hole with patio slabs or bury the inside tub of a washing machine, fill it with garden soil and plant into this. Put the fig somewhere sunny, water it lots during the growing season, do a little pruning and you'll be well rewarded.

Figs are self-fertile and can grow to 2–3m (6–10ft). You can fan or wall-train them, but it's best to keep a pot-grown fig as a short bush. In spring you need to prune out any crossing or damaged branches, and shorten long or bare branches to new growth. In summer, pinch out any new growth leaving just five or six leaves on each branch and no more, this will encourage the small embryonic figs that make next year's fruit to appear. In autumn remove any large figs that have failed to ripen, leaving the small ones to overwinter and ripen next summer. Figs come from warmer climates so protect plants with straw and fleece in winter, or drag the pot under cover for shelter. 'Brown Turkey' is hardy and suitable for our climate.

SOFT FRUIT

STRAWBERRIES

Strawberries are by far the easiest soft fruit to grow, and are at least as happy in a hanging basket as they are in the ground (or even happier as mice and slugs can't get to the fruit and you can move the basket into the sun). To get enough strawberries

Perpetual strawberry plants that I picked up cheap at the market. Perpetual strawberries fruit sporadically in early summer and again in autumn, but don't crop as heavily as summer strawberries.

to make jam you need to fill a space at least 2 x 2m (6 x 6ft), but four hanging baskets will provide enough to garnish cereal, fill a few bowls full or make smoothies. The first season is never prolific, but in years two and three you'll get loads of fruit, then you start again with baby plants. Strawberries send out runners soon after they have fruited, at the end of each is a new plant that you can root in a pot, or in the ground then cut it off from the mother plant. Overwinter baby plants in a coldframe, ready to plant out the following spring.

As strawberries come into flower, place straw under ground-grown plants to stop the fruit rotting on wet ground, and give pot-grown plants a liquid feed to boost growth. Once you've enjoyed all the fruit, cut the plants flush to the ground and compost the leaves and any straw. This stops diseases and a new flush of leaves will soon appear along with hundreds of runners that will be sent out like spiders around the plant. On poor soil, mulch in autumn to help boost growth, otherwise leave well alone until next year's crop.

Strawberries are either early, mid or late season. The earlies appear in June and the late go on into July. Perpetual strawberries, or ever-bearers, crop in June and again in autumn, but not as heavily.

'Hapil' is a midseason upright plant with very sweet fruit. 'Honeoye' is supposed to be very sweet, 'Alice' is an early variety that picks over a long season. 'Rhapsody' is a late season cropper with some resistance to mildews. 'Calypso' bears masses of fruit early in the season and more in early autumn.

RASPBERRIES

Raspberries are soft and easily bruised, which is why they cost a fortune in the shops. Squishing your own raspberries between your fingers to check you have just the right amount of juiciness, that's the point of growing your own – summer-fruiting, autumn-fruiting, or both. Summer-fruiting taste superior, but autumn ones are still tasty, far less fussy and easier to look after. As summer raspberries fruit on the second year's growth, you cut out the old fruiting canes after you've harvested to make room for the young canes to grow up to bear next year's fruit. They need tying in or supporting in some fashion, particularly on windy sites. Mulch in the autumn and wait for next year's crop. Autumn raspberries fruit on this year's growth. All you do to them is cut them to the ground in winter when the canes have died right back and new canes will emerge in spring.

Raspberries have very shallow roots that almost sit on the surface of the soil, so don't weed with a hoe as you'll damage them. I have a variegated mint growing at the base and the pale green of the leaves compliments the pale mint. I've also a very large rhubarb that jollies the raspberries into standing a bit more straight, and neither seem to mind sharing the same space. 'Glen Ample', the almost thornless 'Tulameen', and 'Glen Prosen' are all great summer raspberries for smaller spaces, and 'Autumn Bliss' is the only autumn raspberry worth planting.

BLACKBERRIES, TAYBERRIES, WINEBERRIES, SUNBERRIES, BOYSENBERRIES, LOGANBERRIES AND OTHER HYBRIDS

Blackberries are big beasts, you only need look at their wild siblings to see that. Along with other vigorous hybrids (wineberries are slightly less rampant) they should be planted at least 2.5–3.5m (8–11ft) apart and if they are going against a fence leave a gap between the fence and wires for maintenance. Most hybrid berries fruit in August on two-year-old canes, so you need to train all the new canes into bundles in the middle of your wires or supports, then train them out to the sides – you can make elaborate swirling patterns, or you can just tie the fruiting canes into the lower wires. Once you have finished picking all the fruit, just cut out the spent canes and re-tie this year's canes to the sides.

I'm very fond of some hybrid berries, but they do ramble and grow at such a pace that they may not be the best choice for small gardens. When there are so many wild blackberries to pick for free it seems silly to bother with cultivated blackberries, but you'll never find the fruit of the beautiful Japanese wineberry in shops. They glow in the sun on lovely pink stems covered in prickles so gentle that you can run your hand up them. They also look wonderful on a cold winter's morning. They fruit on last year's canes, but can be managed in small spaces by pinching out the growing tips in spring to make canes branch, giving you more fruit in less space. As long as you can get access to pick, it looks stunning trained along wires at the back of a sunny border.

A tayberry is a cross between a blackberry and a raspberry. It is larger and sweeter than

The first ripe blackberries of the season.

a loganberry, which is also a cross between a blackberry and a raspberry. A boysenberry is a cross between a raspberry, a blackberry and a loganberry. What a promiscuous lot! I'm always excited to come across any of these three, but until I get land enough to home these rampant beasts I'm happy enough to eat raspberries, then wineberries and then wild blackberries (and sometimes all three at once).

BLACKCURRANTS

One healthy blackcurrant bush should produce about 4kg (9lb) of fruit, enough for baking, bottling and puddings. Don't try and pick individual currants, snip off whole sprigs with a pair of scissors. The blackcurrant is quite different from its red and white relatives. It has to be grown as a bush and some large varieties, such as 'Ben Hope', are only good for larger gardens. When you buy currant plants check you're getting certified virus-free stock.

Blackcurrants like rich, well-drained soil in a sunny spot, though they will tolerate partial shade, and they're fine in containers. They flower early in the year, so avoid frost pockets, but they need little attention once established, just an autumn mulch and extra water if the weather is dry when they are beginning to produce fruit. You have to be cruel to be kind when you plant a blackcurrant. Cut back all the stems to one or two buds in the first year, this seems drastic but encourages the roots to go down and new strong shoots to appear. Add plenty of organic matter to the planting hole and leave about 1.5m (5ft) between

Blackcurrants under old net curtains to keep the chickens off.

plants. In the first four years you need only prune out wispy shoots, after that the plant may start to become congested so prune out a third of the oldest growth at soil level to make room for new shoots. Good varieties for small gardens include 'Ben Connan', 'Ben Garin' and 'Ben Sarek'.

GOOSEBERRIES, RED AND WHITE CURRANTS

Gooseberries, red and white currants have similar requirements. Red and white currants are often more prolific than blackcurrants – from a five-year-old bush expect 7kg (15lb) of fruit. Gooseberries will produce 3–4kg (7–9lb) a year. These are all tough, disease-resistant plants that prefer sunny positions, but will happily produce fruit in dappled shade. Grow them as bushes where they will reach a little over 1m (40in) in spread and height, or where space is tight grow

them as cordons or standards (a lollipop of a single tall stem with bushing out on top). This way you can cram a fair amount of fruit in. You will pay about double the price for a cordon bush as a standard, but they're very space-efficient and productive. I'd advise you to buy one already trained, see how it goes and what it looks like, then have a go training a gooseberry or whitecurrant that way. You cannot fault the Royal Horticultural Society's website for detailed information on pruning and training fruit (see Resources page 251). Dig lots of organic matter into the soil before planting any fruit bush and mulch every autumn for good measure. Plant bush types 1–1.5m (3–5ft) apart and cordons 30–40cm (12–16in) apart. Bushes will only need occasional pruning to remove dead, crossing or diseased branches.

Birds love fruit, so you may have to cover plants with netting. I just use old net curtains that I throw on and peg to the plant as the fruit begins to ripen.

'White Grape' and 'White Pear' are both reliable whitecurrants. 'Jonkheer van Tets' is the best redcurrant. Grow 'Invicta' gooseberries for cooking and 'Lord Derby' for large, sweet dessert berries.

BLUEBERRY

I seem to have a long history with blue-berries. My aunt would bring fresh ones in little cardboard containers over from Canada, the minute she was in the door we'd all sit down to blueberries on cornflakes with ice-cold milk. My very first job in horticulture was to look after the Duke of Wellington's blueberries that were grown in a special house just so he too could have them for breakfast on his cereal. And now every garden centre sells them, they are becoming one of the most popular fruit to grow, and for good reason.

There are highbush and lowbush blueberries. Highbush is a larger, more upright plant with prolific, large fruit, the hybrid forms are the predominant commercial types. Lowbush, often called wild blueberries, are short plants with less but intensely-coloured, fruit. Half-high bush hybrids are a cross between the two.

Blueberries are great for containers, where you can provide just the right acidic soil they need. It's still hard to get peat-free compost for acid-loving plants so I plant them in ordinary, good, multi-purpose compost and twice a year mulch with bracken or pine-needles gathered from the less frequented parts of my local park. It's best if you can gather semi-rotted needles and mix with coffee grounds that are naturally acidic. Blueberries need little pruning, only the odd dying branch and perhaps the tips of newly bought plants to increase branching. They naturally grow in very free-draining conditions so add sand to your potting mixture. Water well in dry periods and when the fruit appears pick them quickly before the birds get them. If you have little space fill it with a pot or two of blueberries (you get a better crop if they have friends), maybe underplanted with strawberries.

'Toro' is a mid-season (fruiting in June) highbush with lovely pinkish flowers, good autumn colour, compact habit and juicy fruit. 'Bluecrop' is a slightly larger, very popular highbush with big fruit, don't pick them too early or they're very tart. 'Earliblue' is an early, compact highbush and 'North Country' is a half-high bush that tastes of true wild blueberries.

HONEYBERRY

The honeyberry is a type of honeysuckle. It is relatively new over here, though it's been grown in the States for a while. The fruit is very similar to blueberries, but appears earlier. Although it is a honeysuckle, it doesn't climb and has rather dull flowers. It stays below 1m (40in) and tolerates shade, so is a very good crop for small spaces and the dappled shade of deciduous trees. For pollination you need both *Lonicera caerulea* and *Lonicera caerulea* subsp. *kamtschatica*. They are exceptionally hardy, but hate to sit with wet feet so dig in a good amount of organic matter, homemade compost and give a mulch of compost every autumn. Plant each variety about 1–1.5m (4–5ft) apart and net to keep birds off.

Flowers

Vegetables may be handsome, architectural, beguiling and even beautiful, trees and shrubs may offer seasonal interest, you get to eat fruit and nuts, but it's flowers that hold a garden together.

It's that weave of floral interest that will make your space look more like a garden and less like an allotment.

I love flowers, but unless I had acres of space, I think I'd always see those that you can't eat, don't hold well in a vase or even worse aren't any good for wildlife, well, as pointless. Those man-made double-flowered confectionery specials, such as double polyanthus or overbred bedding-scheme salvias, will never find a home in my edible landscape. I guess if they're your thing then go ahead, but I try to follow the golden rule of William Morris in my garden. There is nothing in it that I do not know to be useful or believe to be beautiful. I define beautiful in terms of wildlife.

My flowers generally fall into one of three categories: I can eat them, the wildlife do very well feeding off them (particularly the local bees) or they make good cut flowers (and presents). I reserve a special category for bulbs and very early spring flowers that offer nectar and pollen for foraging insects when little else is around. The smaller spring flowers are often not great cut flowers and they are mostly inedible, but they offer joy early on and take up little space for the rest of the year.

On the whole, flowers have very different needs to vegetables. Many annual flowers, for instance, do best on poor, free-draining soil. Too much food and they grow leggy, weak and produce soft foliage susceptible to pests and disease. Perennial flowers and annual sunflowers are very demanding on the soil around them, robbing moisture and food from vegetables, but they can exploit soils that are less than ideal for vegetables. Many perennials can take

Previous spread: I'm not sure which is cuter, my dog or the heartsease viola faces.
Opposite: Astrantia major *make excellent cut flowers and are visited by many pollinating beetles and insects.*

quite heavy clay, or very free-draining soils. Granny's bonnet (*Aquilegia vulgaris*) cultivars (good for pollinators), helenium (good for cut flowers), most geraniums, beebalm (*Monarda*) (good for herb tea) and daylilies (*Hemerocallis*) (edible flowers) will all survive clay. Plants for free-draining soils, such as sand, include yarrow (*Alchillea millefolium*) cultivars (good for attracting pollinators), hyssop (*Hyssopus officinalis*) (good for bees and butterflies), and many catmints (*Nepeta*) (loved by bees).

I keep a band of perennial flowers in spaces that are hard to access to harvest vegetables or where the soil is too stony or nutrient-poor for good vegetable growth. Perennial flowers benefit from a mulch in autumn, both to keep down weeds and to slowly break down to supply food for spring growth. I reserve annual flowers for spaces near the path where the soil is very free-draining, or I tuck a few amongst vegetables where each can muddle together well enough. Carrots and annual flowers, such as love-in-a-mist (*Nigella*) make wonderful companions as the love-in-a-mist demands only the very top part of the soil and the carrot can find food deeper down. The same can be said for parsnips, though they will eventually shade out any flowers.

Attractive seedheads on both annuals and perennials should be left over winter, including annual poppies, the native grass *Hordeum jubatum*, cardoons, eryngiums, sunflowers, ice plants (*Sedum spectabile*), and many from the daisy family, such as *Rudbeckias* and asters. They act as shelters for tiny insects and in some cases offer seed for birds. Just before spring appears you can cut back old foliage and seedheads to add

Mouse garlic in flower is edible, covered in bees and has a long vase life.

to the compost. I tend to do this job towards the end of February and have never in my life worried about adding annual flower seeds to the compost. If nature wants to do some seeding around then less work for me.

Large perennial flowers, such as *Sedum autumnale* in my garden, can act as a very large slug and snail hotel. Once they're up and going, many perennials are fairly resistant to slug and snail damage, but can harbour thousands of them under their canopy. It's worth having a hunt before you decide to plant a vegetable next door. But whatever the warnings, I do have two beautiful purple sprouting broccolis that are growing out of perennials. One is surrounded by the valerian *Centranthus alba* that has wrapped its white flowers around it, and the other is nestled into a purple sage. Neither show any signs of unhappiness, have few nibbled leaves and are fine examples of vegetables and flowers being happy enough bedfellows.

BULBS

Bulbs are little things that help themselves and so are perfect for a vegetable-floral weave. Perennials demand a lot of the soil, large annuals compete for moisture and shade out other plants, but bulbs do their thing and then quietly slip away. As long as you allow the leaves to remain, storing up food for next year's flowers, they demand little and offer colour, often when little else is going on. Once the last of the winter veg is floundering and the spring greens have yet to get going, a sweep of small daffodils or a wave of tiny blue flowers is a burst of happiness on cold, grey spring mornings.

Stick to smaller bulbs that can be nestled between plants and have finer, smaller foliage than larger subjects. Small daffodils, such as *Narcissus* 'February Gold' (one the earliest), 'Jenny' (one of the latest) and 'Hawera' (smells good), grape hyacinths, snowdrops, species tulips and scillas are best. *Crocus tomasinianus* is another good subject, as it is very early flowering and has disappeared before the vegetable world has truly begun. Large tulips and daffodils may look good in a vase, but tulips will need replanting year on year to keep up the display and daffodil foliage is a pain to deal with come April, when every spare inch of soil matters. You can always plant some in pots and whip them away when they fade.

Bulbs that go into the ground should be planted deep enough so that you won't disturb them when planting or harvesting, larger bulbs are quite happy planted 12–18cm (5–7in) deep. Pop some around the base of permanent plantings, such as fruit trees, under strawberries and herbs or around the base of cardoons and artichokes. Choose blues or very pale yellows to compliment the grey-blue of emerging spring foliage. *Chionodoxa lucillea* has brilliant blue flowers that face upwards. It will quickly fill in between perennial plants and it works particularly well with globe artichokes, cardoons or as a sea of blue below fruit bushes and trees.

Grape hyacinths (*Muscari*) flower in early March, but the leaves appear as early as October. Plant 5cm (2in) deep about 10cm (4in) apart and allow room for naturalizing. They're a good option for planting under trees, shrubs or roses.

The rich violet-blue flowers of *Scilla bifolia* look good under soft fruit bushes, while *Scilla siberica* is more vigorous and good along path edges or amongst herbs. It also works well in a pot. Plant 5cm (2in) deep.

Tulips and lettuce is a combination that can stop you in your tracks in spring. Plant tulips in autumn and sow winter lettuce (towards the end of September in a coldframe) to plant out as the tulips emerge. *Tulipa* 'Red Riding Hood' is pillarbox red with lovely marked foliage and perfect for small spaces, it also comes back reliably each year. It looks good with 'Winter Density' lettuce.

Smaller species tulips, such as white flowered *Tulipa clusiana*, are particularly good amongst low-growing thyme. And other dainty species tulips such as *T. humilis*, with its bright red flowers, or *T. acuminatea* with its spidery yellow petals look lovely growing through low-growing herbs. Crocus

also work well as their fine foliage won't be in competition.

The wind anemone (*Anemone blanda*) and its many cultivars are best in large drifts under shrubs and trees and happiest in free-draining, but humus-rich soil. Soak them overnight before planting and then plant them about 3cm (1in or more) deep, say 7cm (3in) apart.

Bulbs aren't just for spring, ornamental onions appear from May; they are loved by bees and make very good cut flowers. *Allium moly* is not the showiest of the bunch, the flowers are small compared to its relatives, but it's edible, makes a good cut flower and will make itself at home in dapped shade in rich soil, so is useful for tucking into corners. Both the flowers and bulbs taste mildly of garlic and are nice for salads. *Allium* 'Purple Sensation' has tennis ball sized, deep purple flowers that are excellent cut flowers (if you can bear to cut them). *Allium* 'Globemaster' is another favourite, paler than 'Purple Sensation', but doing the same job. *Allium schubertii* is a wild looking ornamental onion with firework flowers; the dried seed heads make wonderful cut flowers. *Allium cristophii* is another large flower head that works well dried or fresh as a cut flower.

EDIBLE FLOWERS

Clearly edible flowers make perfect sense in an edible landscape. If you are buying container-grown plants in flower then

EDIBLE FLOWERS

SUN LOVERS:

FREE–DRAINING SOILS:

Daisies (flowerbuds and petals so go for the crazy double forms such as 'Bellissimo'). Annual – use as winter bedding for pots, containers and to edge beds. They flower in late autumn to early winter and then again in mid spring.

Nasturtiums. Annual – sow in late spring for summer displays to flower until the first frost.

Calendula. Annual – sow in early spring for summer displays.

Cornflowers (*Centaurea*). Annual – sow in autumn or spring for summer displays.

Sage. Perennial – flowers from midsummer onwards, cut back the flowers before they set seed to get a second flush in late summer.

Rocket. Annual – sow from spring until autumn.

Oriental greens (flowering pak choi, choy sum). Annual – sow from late summer to early autumn.

Pinks (*Dianthus*). Perennial – different forms flower from early summer.

Pelargoniums (lemon scented). Half-hardy perennial – flowers in midsummer.

Jonquil narcissus. Perennial bulb that flowers in late spring, it needs a sheltered, warm spot.

HEAVIER SOILS:

Chrysanthemum greens (often sold as chop suey greens). Annual – sow from spring until autumn, flowers in late autumn.

Rose. Perennial – depending on variety will flower throughout the summer.

Beebalm (*Monarda*). Perennial – flowers in late summer.

Clover. Short-lived perennial – flowers throughout summer.

Daylilies (*Hemerocallis*). Perennial – flowers from early to mid summer.

Sweet Williams (*Dianthus*). Biennial – sow in autumn to flower the following summer.

Hollyhocks. Self-seeding biennial so treat as a perennial – will flower from mid-summer onwards.

Chives. Perennial – flowers sporadically throughout the summer. Eat flowers before they set seed and you'll get a second flush.

DAPPLED SHADE IN MOISTURE-RETENTIVE SOILS:

Many campanulas. Perennial – flowers throughout the summer.

Violets. Perennial – flowers sporadically all year round, won't flower in strong heat.

Mouse garlic. Perennial – flowers in midsummer.

Wild garlic. Perennial – flowers in late spring (also a good foraging plant).

Golden garlic (*Allium moly*). Perennial – flowers in early summer.

Granny's bonnets (*Aquilegia*). Perennial – flowers from late spring to early summer.

Viola 'Rebecca' is perfect for pots and has a long stem for cutting.

consider whether they might have been sprayed with any pesticides, I'd wait till a second flowering before I started picking. Edible flowers are best used as decorative garnish rather than trying to survive on a diet solely of them. They look wonderful in salads or floating on top of soups. Herb flowers, such as chives, sage or rosemary, can be added to oils and vinegars to offer a subtle flavour and enhance their appearance. I always keep a supply in beautiful old bottles for a last-minute unusual gift.

It's best to pick flowers just before serving as many will wilt. You're usually just after the petals, so you can discard the tougher bits. Give them a good blow (or shake) to dislodge any hiding insects before you use them as washing tends to make all the petals stick together.

CUT FLOWERS

A good cut flower is one that will last in a vase. However, you can extend vase life with a few practices. Picking flowers first thing in the morning, rather than in full sun in the afternoon, makes a big difference. If the stems are woody they should be seared in boiling water for 15–30 seconds (the woodier the stem the longer) – the trick is to sear rather than boil the stem. Always use a clean vase and refresh the water every two days to help keep the flowers fresh. If you really want your flowers to last, re-cut the ends (this should be done at an angle with very sharp snips or scissors) every couple of days.

This is cheaper and more environmentally friendly than using those florists sachets that are essentially about stopping bacteria building up in the vase. Flowers that hang their heads down, such as hellebores, look lovely just floating in a saucer of water.

GROWING CUT FLOWERS
I think the trick is to find a balance between flowers and vegetables. I am more interested in growing food than cut flowers, partly because I am greedy, and a little obsessed with the next mouthful. However, there's a whole suite of flowers that make excellent choices for the vase whilst doubling up as very good insect attractors or edible flowers. Some cut flowers do work hard to be allowed space in your garden.

Of course there are anomalies in my garden, plants that can only loosely be said to be good for wildlife and are basically useless in the vase, but you don't have to be totally rigid, this is about gardening not creating a cult.

VIOLAS
Violas are perfect for pots and the front of beds. They need dappled shade to be happy and will tolerate clay. They ramble a bit, nestling themselves in among other plants and popping their heads up into the sun. Certain varieties are bred for cut flowers, you'll have to look to specialist nurseries to find them. Johnny jump-ups or heartsease (*Viola tricolor*), grown in the shade will naturally grow longer stems. The flowers look best as small posies, perhaps a few pin-tucked to a lapel. They are edible and I love to fit them in wherever I can, particularly in pots and next to lettuce. They will grow to 15cm (6in) tall, and 30cm (12in) wide. Sow

in late spring or buy them as plug plants in autumn or spring.

CALENDULA,
(*CALENDULA OFFICINALIS*)
The lovely clear orange flowers of calendula make great cut flowers, the petals are edible, the flowers can make a wonderful skin cream and insects visit as long as the flowers are around, usually right up to the first hard frost in November. Sow in March and space plants about 30cm (12in) apart in full sun, any soil will do. I stuff them towards the front of the border where they do a good job of hiding the bases of kales and brassicas that can get a little bare once you start picking them.

PINKS, (*DIANTHUS* SPP.)
Pinks are particularly good for summer cutting. Old-fashioned border carnations have the longest stems and prefer well-drained soil in full sun. You can eat the flowers and, the more you pick, the more they'll flower. *Dianthus gratianopolitanus* has lovely clove-smelling flowers. I tend to use them in the very free-draining spots next to the path edges where no vegetable would be happy. Buy them in as young plants (look in the alpine section of the garden centre).

PURPLE SAGE, (*SALVIA OFFICINALIS* 'PURPURASCENS')
Every bit of this wonderful evergreen herb is edible – you can make a fantastic pesto out of the flowers – and it's lovely in a vase. Lilac flowers appear in the first half of the summer, contrasting with the deep purple foliage. Grow in moderately fertile, free-draining soil in full sun or light shade. As long as you pick the flowers for cutting

Previous spread: Nasturtium flowers clamber across my Ampersand.

Right: Purple sage in flower. I love this sage for cut flower bouquets and the delicately flavoured flowers are delicious in salads.

you'll keep the plant in shape. I'm using mine to hide the bare bottom of purple sprouting broccoli.

RED VALERIAN,
(*CENTRANTHUS RUBER*)
These flowers are fragrant and either white, pale rose pink or dark crimson. Once it decides it likes your garden it seeds itself around, so pick it for cut flowers to stop the spread. Much loved by foraging insects and pollinators, its leaves are good in a mixed salad. Sow seeds in spring in a coldframe or divide mature clumps carefully in spring. It can grow up to 1m (40in) tall and spreads at least the same distance in free-draining, poor soils, so it's another plant to fill a space that vegetables won't hack.

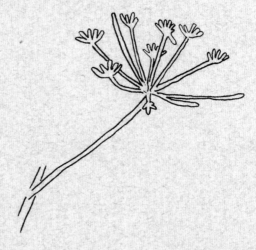

Multi-headed varieties of sunflowers are best for the vase. This one came from a mix called 'Autumn Shades'.

ICE PLANT, (*SEDUM SPECTABILE*)

'September Glow' holds my garden together come autumn. Dense flat flowerheads of deep pink flowers are covered from dawn till dusk in honey bees and other foraging insects. These large flowerheads look stunning in a vase, grouped together with perhaps some *Verbena bonariensis* popping its heads above. They last for a long time, gently fading to antique pink (and can even be dried) and the fleshy leaves are so good in salads it is a must for the garden. Leaves are tangy and fresh tasting, and as they get older they can be fried in a little olive oil. I divide ice plants in spring every three years or so to keep them manageable. They grow in the middle of my beds, and in front of them I have lettuce making the most of the shade they offer at midday, behind I grow broad beans then purple sprouting broccoli and Swiss chard.

LOVE-IN-A-MIST,
(*NIGELLA DAMASCENA*)

Dotted amongst carrots or lettuce, Love-in-a-mist is a delight. It has such fine leaves that it hardly bothers its neighbours, and is very undemanding. It makes a good, long-lasting fresh cut flower and the dried seed heads are very decorative. I sow a lot and save half for the seeds that taste a bit nutmeggy in biscuits and cakes. Grow in full sun in well-drained soil, sowing the seed either in autumn or spring. They will self-seed, but it's easiest just to sow the seeds where you want them.

ANNUAL SUNFLOWERS,
(*HELIANTHUS ANNUUS*)

Sunflowers are jolly, and jolly useful – seed for birds, for you and a wonderful insect plant, although those that are bred for cut flowers tend not to have a great deal of seed. I grow a mixture, some for flowers and some huge ones for seed. Either sow annuals indoors in late winter at 16°C (60°F) in 9cm (3½in) pots and harden them off in a coldframe outdoors for early spring sowing, or sow in mid spring to plant out late spring or early summer. Plant them somewhere sunny. Slugs can be a huge problem with young plants so I tend to pot them on until I have a plant about 30cm (1ft) tall. These seem to withstand attack better when they are planted out. Sunflowers may self-seed, but you'll probably get a mixed bunch as named cultivars rarely come true. Plant them at the back of your border – they make an excellent screen for unsightly fences.

GREEN AMARANTH,
(*AMARANTHUS CAUDATUS*)

'Viridis' is a crazy cut flower with long tassels of green flowers. The leaves and seeds are edible. The leaves are eaten much like spinach and the seeds can be roasted or popped like popcorn. They need hot sun and fairly rich soil, but look very good in a pot where the tassels can hang down. Sow from February to March indoors at 20–25°C (68–77°F) and plant out after the last frost roughly 30cm (12in) apart from any neighbours.

WILD ANGELICA,
(*ANGELICA SYLVESTRIS*)

'Purpurea' is a large perennial and a bit of a statement plant as it grows to 2.5m (8ft) tall and 1m (40in) wide. It has purple flowers that bees love, from July to September, and huge heads of seed from August. The seed is useful in cooking or for tea, and the leaves are good with stewed rhubarb and other acidic fruits. It will tolerate shade or sun, but needs moisture-retentive soil. Sow ripe seed in coldframes on the surface of compost, as it needs light to germinate, and transplant seedlings when they're still young.

DILL, (*ANETHUM GRAVEOLENS*)
Dill is a beautiful annual herb that beneficial insects head for. It tastes fantastic with fish, makes a wonderful tea and is an excellent cut flower. In midsummer it produces flattened umbels of deep yellow flowers. Keep some for seed as this makes a good tea and is also good in cooking. Sow seeds in situ from spring to midsummer to get a succession of fresh foliage and flowers.

Anethum graveolens 'Vierling' has darker blue foliage.

CORNFLOWER, (*CENTUREA CYANUS*)
This is a hardy, edible annual with dark blue flowers from late spring to midsummer. It is great in a vase, the flowers are edible and the petals can make a blue dye for confectionary (if you mash a lot together in a blender and strain them). Sow in the ground or in modules (toilet roll tubes are good as they are biodegradable and avoid root disturbance) in autumn for late spring flowering or in spring for summer flowers.

HELLEBORES, (*HELLEBORUS* SPP.)
Hellebores are my weakness, my anomaly, a plant that I'm shamelessly in love with. Perhaps not the best cut flower, though a bowl full of floating flowers in late winter is a joy, and they are visited by early foraging bees, but for me they need no justification. A garden without hellebores, well, it wouldn't be my garden. They are woodland plants and grow best in dappled shade in rich, moisture-retentive soils. I plant mine around the bases of fruit trees, under rambling roses and I have a lovely spring combination of white Swiss chard and hellebores. They are a promiscuous lot and will rapidly hybridize and seed themselves around. If possible, add some leaf mould when planting and mulch in the autumn.

AND A FEW MORE
It turns out I have more than one weakness ... asters. New England aster (*Aster novae-angliae*), *Aster amellus*, *Aster* x *frikartii* are wonderful, late-flowering perennials that make a garden and make an even finer cut flower. Much loved by bees and insects, they need sun or very partial shade. Mulch them well in spring after cutting back the foliage and divide them every three to five years in spring to keep plants vigorous. *Verbena bonariensis* is a very upright perennial with minute foliage and extremely long stems, topped with lilac-purple flowers. It is often referred to as a see-through plant as it doesn't obscure anything behind it, so you can dot it all over the place. It flowers on and on from mid summer to early autumn, it's good for insects and great for holding a garden together. I have a lovely combination of verbena and 'Red Russian' kale (and below them deep purple violas) at the bottom of the garden.

BOUQUETS

BIRTHDAY BOUQUETS

A homegrown bouquet is a lovely gift, and if you can eat it or dry it for future use, so much the better.

Globe artichokes.

THE GOURMET BOUQUET

- Globe artichoke (pick the artichoke ready to eat rather than in flower as the *pièce de résistance* of the arrangement).

- Purple sage.

- Love-in-a-mist seedheads.

- Marjoram in flower, but with enough leaves to be useful.

- Garlic scapes – unopened garlic flowers – are quite a delicacy.

- *Viola* 'Rebecca'.

THE HOUSE-WARMING HERB BOUQUET

A mixture of the following will dry perfectly. The idea is to provide some of the most useful herbs until the owner gets their own garden going.

- Rosemary.

- Bay.

- Sage.

- Thyme.

- Winter savory.

- Oregano.

- Chive or lavender flowers.

Opposite: An almost edible bouquet. You can't eat the red heleniums but the rest can go straight to the pot. Above: A herb bouquet.

Seed Saving

When you've grown masses of your own produce, it makes complete sense to save some seeds to grow on next year, rather than starting afresh and buying in new seeds each year.

If you're unsure about saving your own to start with, at least make sure that you save unused seed from bought-in seed packets, rather than chucking away what you don't use.

HOW TO SAVE AND STORE SEEDS

As soon as you open a foil-sealed seed packet you expose the seeds to temperature and moisture levels and the seed will begin to decline. How long you can keep your seeds depends on how you decide to store them. The best possible place to store your seeds is an airtight container, either in your fridge or your freezer (remember your seeds can survive as low as -80°C (-112°F)). If you use your freezer you do need to slowly acclimatize them by moving them to the fridge first and then outdoors before you open the container to sow them. I store some of my most precious seed in the freezer as a back-up, then I store some of this year's seed in the fridge and the rest live in a box in a relatively cool, dark cupboard. The quickest way to kill seed is to leave it on a warm windowsill, out in the sun or in a greenhouse.

If you get hold of any little sachets of silica gel that come inside packaging to keep moisture out, keep these for seed storing. Place them in a cool cooling oven, so that they dry out, and then use them in your seed box.

HOW TO DO A SEED GERMINATION TEST

If you've had seed sitting around for a while there's a simple test to see how viable the seed still is. Dampen several pieces of kitchen towel and

Previous spread: Mexican ground cherry husks begin to swell and ripen for picking in October.
Opposite: Radish seedpods are an edible delicacy, but radish are promiscuous and won't come true from seed.

spread some of your seed, say 10 per cent of however many seeds you have, between the kitchen towels. Place them in a clear plastic bag and put it somewhere warm (on top of the fridge or in an airing cupboard). After a week or two you should see signs of germination. You're not looking for a full seedling, just the beginning of life – the first root poking out, perhaps a little green. The percentage of your specimens that germinate is a very rough guide to how well the rest of the packet will germinate. If you have 80 per cent germination sow a few more seeds than you would normally need. If its down to 50 per cent you're going to have to sow double the amount, but if it's less than 50 per cent I'd probably compost it.

HOW TO SAVE YOUR OWN SEED

It makes good sense to save some of your own seed. Firstly you'll save money, particularly if you're saving for microgreens and cut-and-come-again crops where you need a lot of seed. It also makes good environmental sense as you will be helping to preserve genetic diversity and you can save heritage varieties that are no longer sold by commercial seed houses. The Heritage Seed Library is one organization that offers a cornucopia of vegetables specific to locations and periods to its members. Older seed may do better on your site than a lot of new commercial seed as seeds used to be grown for particular places. Names like 'Kenilworth' tomato or 'Cheltenham' green top beetroot are testament to a time when seeds had a locality. They have history to them and flavour from the past.

Broad bean 'Red Epicure' seeds for next year.

Currently we rely on just a few multi-national seed companies for most of our seeds. Many newer seeds are genetically very similar to each other and many are F1, which means their seeds cannot be used. There are many excellent F1 hybrid plants, but open-pollinated seed (seed that is bred true to variety and is pollinated by nature, be it by bees, wind or other insects) offers all growers the same potential crop, no-one can own the rights because the seed hasn't been modified, and it ensures a necessary genetic diversity.

A lot of the latest commercial seed is produced for growers, not gardeners. Growers want plants that mature at the same time, have a uniform colour and size and often plants that can be mechanically picked and processed. As a gardener, you want almost the opposite. It makes sense to have varieties that will crop over a long period, rather than ones that offer a glut in August. Older varieties often offer flavour over size.

If you save seed that does particularly well on your site year on year it will slowly adapt specifically to your part of the world. No commercial seed house is going to breed and test for a plant specifically so it does well on say, a wet, windy allotment in Wales, but if you find a bean that does, keep hold of it. It doesn't necessarily take a long time, garlic will show local adaptation within a few growing seasons.

Unfortunately, older seed is constantly being lost from seed catalogues as the newest variety comes out and takes its place, this is why we see so little diversity in the supermarket. Yet diversity is key, as being

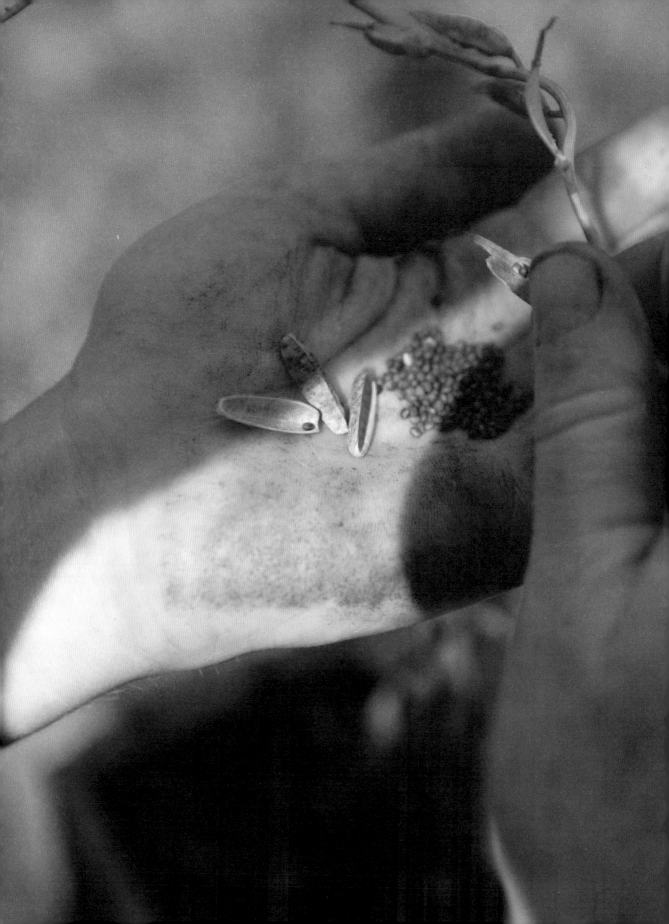

Ripe rocket seed.

reliant on so few seeds is risky, we need as many different strains of seed as possible. It is far better to constantly cultivate old seed varieties rather than saving them up in a genebank that relies on investment that might not always be available. Every time you save even just a few seeds you are contributing towards biodiversity.

Some seeds are very easy to save. Rocket will happily seed itself around, doing the work for you. So will violas, poppies, buckwheat, land cress, lamb's lettuce and chrysanthemum greens. You can just leave these to flower and seed and let nature do the rest. Other seeds require a little more help, as they will cross-pollinate with other family members if left to their own devices (brassicas, courgettes, pumpkins and squashes are notorious for this). These plants need to be isolated at some distance from each other so that they don't cross-pollinate with other varieties of the same family – a cabbage crossed with a broccoli is quite possible, but would be useless to the gardener except as a curiosity.

You may need to save from a number of individual plants to get enough variability in the seeds, and you'll have to wait a long time to save seed from some plants – carrots are biennial so they don't produce seed for a year or two and so it may tie up your space for too long to get the seed.

Some seed is easy to save and anyone can try. If you want to know more, the ins and outs of saving different species are quite specific so go to Resources (page 251) and check out two brilliant works on how to go about becoming your own seed bank.

ROGUEING

Rogueing is literally getting rid of rogue plants. Whatever seed you save should be grown the next year to make sure you are only saving healthy plants. Remove any that are mottled, distorted or that look weak or show signs of disease. Or that just look too different from the normal type. The point is to save specific characteristics. If you save, say, a pea that's known for a certain flower colour, to save any that are not true to type will mean slowly degrading the desirable characteristic.

EASY SEED SAVERS

ROCKET
I save the seed of the last plants to flower. These tend to overwinter and flower in spring. I harvest the seed when the seed head has gone buff-coloured and is fat and firm. I hang the seedhead upside down over a bucket and let it dry, pop open and the seed fall out. There is a natural, post-harvest dormancy of two months, so don't sow the seed immediately.

LETTUCE
You can save off just one or two plants of lettuce as they are naturally strong inbreeders (naturally self-pollinated), but never save seed from self-seeders. You get thousands of seeds from just one plant, but ideally you should save about ten plants with rogueing in mind. It is a good idea to have about 2m (6ft) between different varieties.

Do not save plants that bolt first as you will just increase this habit in future generations. If you are saving more than one variety, then you will need to take precautions against cross pollination by separating plants by about 2m (6ft), preferably with something tall growing in between.

Lettuce seed ripens over a period of time, so the best way to collect it is by shaking the seed heads daily into a brown paper bag. The seeds will need cleaning up to remove them from their seed capsules. They can be gently rubbed through a sieve to remove the largest debris.

PEAS

Peas are also strong inbreeders, so you don't need a lot of plants – between five and ten – and they don't tend to cross-pollinate so you won't need to isolate different varieties. Rogue out any distorted, small or weak plants as these may have seed-borne diseases.

Leave pods to dry on the plant. When they have turned buff and rattle you should take them inside, shell the seeds out of the pods and allow them to dry further. Remove any seeds with small holes, as this is a sign of the pea moth that will eat the seed from inside, and then pupate in the soil. Discard any odd coloured or very small seeds.

BEANS

Runner and French beans are very easy to save, you just leave them on the plant until they rattle. However, they are fairly difficult to keep true to strain as they will readily cross-pollinate with other climbing beans that you or your neighbours are growing. In order to keep a variety true you will have to isolate the plants by at least 100m (330ft) or bag individual flower trusses and hand pollinate. Or you could just eat the beans over winter instead!

The wild rocket (the yellow flower) seeds itself around my garden doing half the work for me.

SAVE FOR CUT-AND-COME-AGAIN CROPS

If you are saving brassicas for microgreens (eating the plants at seedling stage) you don't have to worry too much about their promiscuous nature. Kales and loose-headed cabbage that overwinter are the easiest to save from. These will naturally start to set seed in spring and the only trick is to harvest the seed before the birds get to it. Covering the seedheads in horticultural fleece pegged down with clothes pegs works fine.

Seeds should be completely dry before storage. You can tell if a seed is dry as it tends to snap rather than bend, or in the case of a bean or pea it should be so hard that your nail doesn't leave an impression if you dig it into the seed. Store seeds in paper envelopes or look out for wage packets at the stationers. You can also find some DIY seed packet designs online, these make nice presents when you add your own touches.

REAPING YOUR HARVEST

You've got some of the world's finest ingredients at your fingertips, now's the time to get down to some real cooking. Here are some of my favourites, a few suggestions that may be new to you, and some great pictures to inspire you to go create.

Harvesting

The best way to harvest is little and often.

This way you don't get overwhelmed by a giant amount of produce and you can process the food in small, manageable batches, rather than having to stop everything to bottle and freeze madly for several days. Polyculture lends itself to gradual harvesting, you pick lots of greens at seedling stage – such as radish leaves or baby salads – and unless you grow exclusively F1 hybrids that tend to mature at exactly the same time, harvesting any one crop will happen over a period of time as some plants grow faster than others.

However, courgettes, French and runner beans and cucumbers have a way of catching up on you. You don't need to fall into the trap of thinking you need supermarket-long cucumbers or yard-long beans. Pick often, pick tender and you'll end up picking over a longer period.

If you have too much of any one thing get lots of people round, make jam or bottle tomatoes and share out the produce as a thank-you for taking part.

BOTTLED LOVE: BOTTLING AND PRESERVING

JAMS AND JELLIES

There are sensible reasons to make jam, it's one of the best ways to preserve a surplus of soft fruit, homemade jam is economical and you can make flavours you'd never find in the shops. I make jam because it is part of my history, like making bread and sloe gin. I preserve not just fruit but memories, place and identity with every jar. Mostly I make jam with my girlfriends so it becomes something else, too: gossip, community and sharing. I am happy when I've got a cupboard full of jam.

Sugar, pectin and acid are required to set and bring out the flavour of any jam. Cooking apples, crab apples, black- and redcurrants, damsons, gooseberries, plums and rhubarb are all high in acid and pectin so they make good setting jam. Medium setters include apricots, blackberries (though they lose their pectin as the season progresses), gages, loganberries and raspberries. Fruits that struggle to set on their own include cherries, pears and some strawberries. These

need either to be paired with a good setter, (which is why many recipes call for crab apples, cooking apples or acid such as lemon juice), or need to be cooked with sugar that has pectin added or Certo (a liquid apple pectin). But watch out, to have perfectly set jam isn't everything and you can ruin the flavour with too much pectin.

THE GOLDEN JAM RULES

Buy a jam pan. Good jam comes down to having a good jam pan. Use it and love it, jam pans are good for more than just preserving. For every 600ml of fruit pulp you need 450g of sugar (1 pint to 1lb if you are following my mother's recipe). Many jam pans have litres and pints measured up the side, another reason to love them!

To make jam you just remove the stones, but to make jelly you have to strain the pulp so that all you are left with is liquid. You can buy jelly bags or use muslin folded several times. Or you can use a pair of cheap tights. An old pillowcase (ironed to sterilize) makes a very good strainer for jellies. It is very important when making jelly not to squeeze the contents as this impairs the clarity of your jelly.

The sugar content of jam is very important – sugar not only brings out the taste, it preserves the fruit. You need 60 per cent of the final weight of the jam to be sugar in order for the jam to be preserved (the pint for pound rule). All fruit should be cooked until soft before the sugar is added. You can use either beet or cane sugar (I grappled with this ethical and environmental nightmare as it's hard to get organic beet sugar, but cane sugar comes from half way around the world ...). The size of the sugar crystals determines how clear the jam looks and how much scum you get. Granulated sugar gives you more scum. Sugar can make the skins of some fruits harder, if damsons, for example, aren't properly softened before the sugar is added then they toughen up and there is little you can do about this. The rule is: slow cooking before the sugar and very rapid, short cooking afterwards.

You can tell if your jam has set by using the cold plate test. Allow a teaspoon of jam to cool on a cold plate; the surface should crinkle when you push it with a finger, but don't leave the jam boiling while you check or you may miss the setting point. You finish it off by allowing it to cool a little, so that any scum collects on the top, which you remove quickly with a clean, slotted spoon. Wait until the end to remove the scum or you'll lose a lot of jam.

Pour your jam into perfectly clean, dry and warm (not hot or you'll burn the jam) jars. You can sterilize your jars in boiling water for five minutes or in the oven. Heat your oven to 140°C (280°F), leave it for five minutes then turn it off and put in the jars for 10–15 minutes. Fill them right to the top with jam, because it shrinks as it cools, but if you have whole fruit you need to let the jam cool a little until there is a skin in the pan and then slowly stir the jam and pour it gently into the jars. If you don't do this all the fruit will rise to the top – and you won't be allowed to join the WI!

Before you put the lids on you need to gently press a disc of waxed paper on top of each pot of jam. This prevents mould forming, or if any does form it rarely penetrates past the paper. I put the lids on while the jam is hot to make a tight seal.

Top l-r: Straining Oregon grape jelly in a jelly bag. Testing the setting point in jam or jelly.

Bottom l-r: Jams and jellies shrink as they cool so fill right to the top. Use greaseproof paper on top of the jam to stop mould.

BLACKBERRY AND APPLE JAM OR JELLY

1¾kg (4lb) of blackberries

750g (1½lb) of cooking apples or wild crabapples

300ml (½ pint) of water

2¼kg (5lb) of sugar

You need a jelly bag or similar to strain the fruit

Very ripe blackberries can be low in pectin and are difficult to wash so try and pick slightly unripe ones. I think the smaller wild berries have a better flavour than the large ones. Wash the berries and place them in your jam pan with half the water and simmer until tender. Core, peel and dice the apples and simmer in a separate pan with the remaining water until also tender (the apples need longer to cook). Stir the fruit together and strain the mixture through a nylon sieve or jelly bag. Although you get less jam, seedless blackberry jam is much, much better. Return the strained fruit to the pan with the sugar and stir until dissolved. Bring to the boil and boil rapidly until setting point is reached. Pour into clean, dry, warm jars and seal.

RASPBERRY JAM

Unless you add a teaspoon of citric acid (or 2 tablespoons of lemon juice) this jam will not set very firm. I like it unadulterated, melting on hot toast, but it's up to you.

1kg sugar to every kg of raspberries (or 1 pound of sugar to every pound of raspberries)

Unlike other jams, you need to heat the sugar and raspberries together very slowly, either by mixing the jam and sugar and putting your pan in a very low oven for a while or just stirring very gently over a low heat. When the sugar has dissolved, give the mixture a good hard stir to make sure there is no sugar lurking at the bottom and then boil very hard for several minutes. You will reach a setting point quickly. Pot as usual.

WILD JAMS

DAMSON CHEESE

Wash the fruit and just cover with water. Bring to the boil and simmer until the fruit is soft. Rub the fruit through a sieve to remove the skin and stones then measure the resulting pulp. You'll need 450g of sugar to 600ml of pulp (a pound of sugar to every pint of pulp). Return to the pan and stir in the sugar until it dissolves, then boil for around 45 minutes, stirring constantly. Setting point is reached when you can stir through the jam and leave a trail showing in the bottom of the pan, it should be thick, but still easy to stir. Quit after 45 minutes as you'll be there. Remove from the heat and pour into moulds or jam jars with wide openings so you can cut out chunks of cheese. Damson cheese is excellent with sharp, hard cheese or cut into cubes and eaten a bit like Turkish delight.

Damson cheese is perfect with rice pudding or yoghurt.

OREGON GRAPE JAM (*MAHONIA AQUIFOLIUM*)

You often find these berries in parks or front gardens from August to September. The berries are bitter if you eat them raw, but rich in acids, though you'll still need to add pectin to the jam.

Either add the juice of one lemon to every 900g (2lb) of fruit or a teaspoon of citric acid. You'll need to sieve or strain the pulp (you can squeeze this one) and add 450g of sugar for every 500ml of fruit (a pound of of sugar to 1 pint of fruit). Stir the sugar in and boil for around 20 minutes until setting point is reached. Bottle as usual.

ROWAN JELLY (*SORBUS AUCUPARIA*)

Consider this to our British larder what cranberry jelly is to the States and eat it with game and meat. I think it's by far the most beautiful of all wild jams and has a distinctly tart flavour. You don't need to go mad picking the berries (they are best towards the end of September, then they go mushy and the birds get them) as a couple of jars is plenty for most store cupboards. You'll need some crab apples to help the rowans set. They're often found growing near rowans, but if you can't find any, use cooking apples.

Remove the stalks and wash the fruit. Add just enough water to cover the berries and simmer until all the fruit is tender. Strain through a jelly bag or an old pillowcase, leaving the pulp overnight strung between two chairs if necessary. Do not squeeze the contents. Measure the liquid and to every pint add a pound of sugar (450g of sugar to 500ml of fruit). Dissolve the sugar slowly and then bring to a rapid boil until setting point is reached. Bottle or jar as normal.

PICKLES: ONE NIGHT, THREE WEEKS AND THE REST OF YOUR LIFE

ONE-NIGHT PICKLES

Ichiyazake are 'overnight pickles' that are a common part of Japanese cuisine where salt and weight are used to draw the water out from vegetables. You can make this in the morning to serve that evening or overnight. The vegetables will last for about two days in the fridge.

Spicy green leaves such as mizuna, radish, mustard or turnip leaves, or slices of cucumber
Salt
Chillies or togarashi (a blend of dried chillies, sesame, pepper, seaweed and ginger)

Wash the leaves and sprinkle them with salt. If the leaves are tough or have prominent midribs then massage the salt in a little with your fingers. You'll need a bowl large enough to fit a plate inside. Layer the leaves adding chilli to every other layer (but don't use it on spicy mustard or radish leaves) and sprinkle more salt on top of the last layer. Place the plate on top to weigh down the vegetables. Use a pan or glasses filled with water as weights, or use a large

scrubbed and boiled stone. After 12 hours wash the pickles to remove the salt, wring them out and slice them up. One-night pickles can turn a dull rice and vegetable dish into something sublime.

SOUR DILL PICKLES

Sour dill pickles, to me, say New York deli and are particularly good in a cheese sandwich served in a dinner roll (bread made with buttermilk).

These pickles use fermentation in brine rather than vinegar to preserve the cucumbers, so they won't keep for much more than a month in the fridge – I can't tell you exactly how long as we eat them so quickly.

Proper sour dill pickles use small gherkins pickled whole. I use any cucumbers or gherkins I have grown and usually slice them as they take longer to go sour if left whole. Cucumber can be too soft, especially if they're not picked young. One way around this is to add fresh grape leaves to preserve the crunch and stop the whole thing turning to mush.

These pickles take anything from three days to four weeks to ferment. There are two things that seem to affect the speed of pickling, the ambient temperature of the room you pickle them in (try and keep them out of the sun) and whether they're chopped or pickled whole. I slice mine and they ferment very quickly. You have to keep tasting them to work out how sour you like them. Once they are at the right stage,

place a lid on top and pop them straight into the fridge to slow down the fermentation process.

The more salty the brine, the more sour the taste – add about three tablespoons of salt in every litre (2 pints) of water for a strong sour taste or two tablespoons for less sour.

10–15 small cucumbers/gherkins or 3 large ones, sliced
2 bay leaves, crumbled
3 cloves of garlic, peeled
A pinch of bruised peppercorns
2 tablespoons chopped dill (dried or, better still, fresh and just starting to set seed)
2–3 tablespoons sea salt
1 litre (2 pints) water
Kilner jar or similar glass bottle

Dissolve the salt in the water (if necessary heat it then cool it down). Sterilize your glass jar and leave to cool. Pack the cooled jar with layers of cucumber, dill, garlic, peppercorns and bay. Cover with brine. You need to make sure that the cucumber remains covered in brine. I use a mug filled with water to weigh down the contents and if the brine doesn't cover the contents when they're weighted down I add more brine.

Cover with a tea towel or muslin cloth to keep flies out. After several days a scum may appear around the rim. If this happens skim this off and rinse the weight before replacing it.

BREAD AND BUTTER PICKLES AND OTHER VINEGAR-BASED PICKLE RECIPES

Bread and butter pickles are the opposite of sour pickles, they're sweet and vinegary. My mother makes them by combining white wine vinegar with at least a cup of sugar, a pinch of mustard seeds, several cloves of garlic (sliced), perhaps some chillies and lots of sliced cucumbers. Her recipe is done mostly by taste. If the vinegar is too sour, she adds sugar. She heats the vinegar and sugar together in a pan before pouring over the packed jars of cucumbers. These are delicious and everyone in the family eats them up before you can even say winter store cupboard.

MY MOTHER'S RECIPE

1 large cucumber

1 medium sized onion, peeled and sliced very thinly in rounds

1 green chilli, deseeded and sliced in rounds

½ teaspoon sea salt

450ml (¾ pint) white wine vinegar

Sour dill pickles in the first stage of fermentation.

225g (8oz) caster sugar, or to taste

1–2 cloves of garlic, peeled and sliced thinly

1 tablespoon mustard seeds

1 tablespoon celery seeds

1 tablespoon chopped dill

1 stick of cinnamon bark (optional)

6 juniper berries (optional)

More chilli (optional)

Peel and cut the cucumber into thin discs. Mix in a bowl with the salt, chillies, garlic and onion. Heat the vinegar, sugar and spices together in a saucepan until the sugar has dissolved. Add the vegetables to the saucepan and bring to a gentle simmer. Spoon into hot, sterilized jars and seal. Store somewhere cool.

SOIL SISTER PICKLES

The Soil Sisters are Daphne Lambert and Miche Fabre Lewin. It's safe to say they are both very passionate about food, the soil and the well-being of the body and the planet. They care deeply about every morsel that goes into your mouth. Their recipes are based around local, seasonal artisan food.

When I met the Soil Sisters they made a version of bread and butter pickles that was ultra healthy and, dare I say it, even better than my mother's. Instead of heating white vinegar and sugar together, they combine cider vinegar with apple juice concentrate. Apple juice concentrate is very sweet, but when it's combined with the vinegar you get a wonderful, rich fruity sweet-and-sour thing going on.

I've played around and tried balsamic with red grape juice and white wine vinegar with white grape juice, both of which worked well, but the apple thing blows them both away.

For the solution, mix the vinegar and juice concentrate together in a bowl until you get the right sweet/sour ratio. Then add herbs or spices and let everything sit so the flavours combine. As you chop your vegetables put them straight into the solution to marinate. Once you've finished chopping pack everything in a jar. If there is not enough solution top up with more vinegar and juice concentrate (make it in a bowl first to get the ratio right, rather than just pouring it straight in). All the vegetables must be covered in vinegar as this is how they are preserved, any exposed to the air will quickly ruin. If your vegetables keep floating to the top it's just because you haven't packed enough into the jar, it doesn't need to be airtight. If you are using a metal lid place a disc of waxed paper underneath it to prevent the acid corroding it.

You can start eating these pickles straight away, but they do improve with age. Once the jar is opened it's best to keep it in the fridge, but an unopened jar can keep for several years.

SOIL SISTER-INSPIRED PICKLES

450ml (¾ pint) cider vinegar
50ml (2 fl oz) apple juice concentrate (you may need more if you want a sweeter taste)
2 teaspoons salt
450g (1lb) green beans, strung and sliced
2 cloves of garlic, peeled and sliced
1 habenero chilli, deseeded and sliced
1 x 5cm (2in) piece of cinnamon bark
A couple of bay leaves
A small sprig of winter savory
A pinch of black peppercorns

You can play around with other herbs and spices such as rosemary, juniper berries, red perilla (to add a bit of colour), Dulce seaweed (a low-salt alternative) and chive flowers.

These pickles keep best in the fridge.

CHUTNEY

The difference between a chutney and a pickle is that chutneys are cooked in vinegar and pickles aren't. Chutneys are made by combining any two or more vegetables or fruit. You're basically aiming for a sweet/sour and perhaps hot combination. Onions are nearly always added, often mustard seeds, chillies, apples, raisins and tomatoes are too. Chutneys are a great way to use up a glut, but go easy on how much you make, it's quite easy to have too many 'vintage' chutneys from last year and the year before hanging around.

The great thing about chutney is that once you get the basic premise sorted you can add all kinds of ingredients. I made a batch called chocney last year, which was a green tomato chutney that got a bit burnt as I neglected to pay attention to the pot. I'd heard that you could add dark chocolate to take away the burnt flavour from stews, but didn't know exactly how much. I put in half a large bar (it turns out you just need a square). The result, however unconventional, came out as an amazing, Mexican-style 'mole-type' side dish.

GREEN TOMATO CHUTNEY

Green tomato chutney is one of the most useful recipes as it doesn't matter if the summer sun fails or blight gets your plants. As long as you can pick some healthy, firm fruit you can make something to show for your hard labour.

1¾kg (4lb) green tomatoes, diced into cubes (if you are using cherry tomatoes leave them whole)

2 large onions (red is best), or 450g (1 pound) shallots, peeled and diced

200g (7oz) raisins, dried cranberries or dried blueberries

15g (½oz) root ginger, finely chopped

8–10 chillies (deseeded if you don't want the chutney to be too hot), chopped

450g (1lb) apples, peeled, cored and chopped

2 tsp salt

450g (1lb) brown sugar

2 teaspoons peppercorns

6 cloves of garlic, peeled and sliced

600ml (1 pint) malt vinegar, or red wine vinegar if you use red onions

Place all the ingredients in a large, thick-bottomed pan (it must have a thick bottom otherwise you'll spend a lot of time stirring to stop the bottom from burning). Heat gently, stir often and simmer until the ingredients blend together into a rich pulpy mass with a fairly thick consistency. Pour into jars and seal.

DRYING

DAMSONS AND PLUMS

Spread the damsons or plums out over a baking tray covered with baking parchment and sprinkle with a little sugar. Set your oven on its lowest heat and bake the damsons until they no longer give off any liquid – this takes between four and six hours. Some fruit will be more dry than others, so you then need to put it all into a large glass jar with a lid and leave it for a few days, shaking the jar several times a day to distribute the moisture.

You may want to pasteurize the fruit to kill any insects' eggs (particularly fruit flies) or bacteria. Seal the dried fruit in a thick freezer container (not bags) and freeze for 48 hours. Remove and immediately package for permanent storage in a glass jar. Don't leave them to sweat in the freezer container or they'll reabsorb moisture.

I have both stoned the fruit and left it whole. Stoned damsons basically shrink down to their skins, so there's not much of them, but they just taste so good.

APPLE RINGS

Use sweet dessert apples rather than cookers. Once I've finished my own apples I buy apples from the farmers' markets and continue to make apple rings all winter. They're the ultimate in low-calorie moreish snack food.

Remove the core of the apples and slice them into rings 5mm (¼ in) thick. Remove any bruised parts and soak the slices for ten minutes in a citric acid solution made of 1 teaspoon acid to 400ml (¾ pint) of cold water. This stops the apple rings from discolouring and also has an antimicrobial effect. You don't have to peel, however peeled rings may take slightly longer to dry. I thread my rings onto a clean, oiled (use vegetable oil, it will stop the rings from sticking) bamboo cane and hang it above a radiator, or you can dry them on racks in a very low oven. Oven drying takes six hours, over a radiator takes about three days. A dry apple ring should feel a bit like

chamois leather and several rings pressed together should spring apart (rather than stick to each other). It's a good idea to further condition the rings and pasteurize as for damsons, then store in an airtight container out of the sun. They can last from 6–12 months.

FREEZING

Almost all vegetables should be blanched before freezing by scalding them in boiling water to stop certain enzyme actions, which can cause loss of flavour, colour and texture. It also helps stop the loss of vitamins. Different vegetables need different times, mostly between two and five minutes in the water. Blanching for too long is worse than not blanching at all. However, I don't blanch courgettes, but instead shred them, squeeze out excess moisture and bag into freezer bags.

Beetroot, pumpkin and winter squash can't be frozen fresh, but need to be fully cooked before freezing.

Green beans need to be blanched for three minutes. I slice mine diagonally or put them through a stringer first.

Carrots need to be peeled and diced or cut into rounds and blanched for two minutes.

Broccoli needs to be blanched for three minutes for a small head, up to five minutes for large heads.

SOFT FRUIT

Blackberries, raspberries, gooseberries and currants all freeze very well. Spread the fruit out on trays and let them freeze separately, then pack them into freezer bags once frozen. I find that frozen fruit is

Slice the apple rings about a quarter of an inch thick and soak in citric acid solution. Hoop them on oiled bamboo canes to stop the rings from sticking. They will take several days to dry. Store in an airtight container.

easier to wash than fresh, so I just take out what I need and wash them quickly before they defrost.

HERBS

Your herbs need to be picked at their peak. Look for good colour and only freeze healthy plants. It's easiest to freeze a few sprigs or leaves at a time. Wash, drain and pat dry with a towel. Place in freezer bags, seal and freeze. Once they are frozen you can crumble them up in order to get more into a bag (have one bag for initial freezing and one for the crumbled herbs). Use these herbs in cooking, they discolour and go limp on defrosting so they're no good for garnishing. Basil looks particularly horrid, as it goes black, so I prefer to freeze it pre-chopped and covered in oil then put into ice cube trays.

CHILLIES

Deseed, slice and freeze in freezer bags.

Raspberry 'Autumn bliss' for freezing.

Home Cooking

Putting the season into your food.

For me growing and cooking food is one of the best ways to express how much I care about those who eat with me. I cannot wrap love up in a better way than to serve up a dish that I have laboured over to grow and then processed into a good supper, a jar of jam or just a good drink to end the day on.

When people talk about civilization they often point to galleries, fine paintings and grand architecture, but they miss out one vital example, soil. Soil is our civilization and from that soil, our food. Ever since the wild food of our ancestors we have bred a rich heritage of taste. The labour and struggle to grow better-tasting fruit and vegetables has taken millennia and involved thousands of gardeners across different continents and in different cultures. It has often been hard labour, especially when losing a crop meant more than just disappointment.

There is only one way to halt the decline in taste and variety that the last decades have brought us, and that is to serve up our own homegrown food, bravely and boldly. When I rummage through the potato store, deciding whether I want to serve blue, red, pink or white potatoes, I'm not just thinking of my harvest, but of the heritage of humankind. Growing and eating my own food is my way of holding onto the past whilst (hopefully) ensuring a better future.

What follows is a smattering of recipes passed down, borrowed or adapted from friends and family. These are dishes that I return to when I am too tired for an adventure and just need something honest and wholesome for our plates.

SPRING

NETTLE SOUP

I tend to pick about a carrier bag's worth of tips to make a soup big enough to feed six, or I pick more and make several batches for the freezer, because come summer nettle leaves are too tough to pick.

It's best to pick nettle leaves in washing up gloves and make sure you pick from

Previous spread: A pickling still life: wild walnuts, wobbly French beans and a gherkin.

plants that haven't been peed on. You really want to only pick the tips (the first 5cm) as lower down the leaves are too tough.

A carrier bag of nettle tips – very carefully washed, grit is not a good ingredient

1 large potato, diced

1 leek (if you have one handy), chopped into rounds

1 large onion, diced

2 large cloves of garlic, minced

750ml (1½ pints) stock (I usually use chicken)

Water to top up with

2–3 tablespoons crème frâiche

Salt and pepper to taste

Sauté the onions until golden and translucent for around eight minutes, add the garlic, leeks and potato and cook for another five minutes, or until the vegetables are just beginning to soften. Add the stock and nettles and cook for 20 minutes, or until the nettles are soft. Top up with more water if necessary and season to taste. Now blend the whole mixture and add enough crème frâiche to turn it a pale mint green colour.

I've substituted many other wild foods – for example, when ransoms appear I use them instead of garlic. I sometimes add garlic mustard at the last minute and I also use all sorts of other greens, such as ground elder or dead nettles, adding lemon juice to give the soup a tang.

JAPANESE KNOTWEED SPEARS

Once you've tasted these you'll never look at this weed the same way.

Pick these like asparagus (please, please make sure that no one has sprayed them with herbicides first). You want emerging tips the size of your thumb with fat rather than hollow stems. Sautéed in olive oil and dressed with a little salt and lemon they're heaven. Whipped up with eggs for a frittata is genius, or use them in a cream sauce with a little horseradish.

SCAFATA

Scafata is an Umbrian stew made with fresh broad beans, tomatoes and some sort of late winter green, either a chicory or (my favourite) baby Swiss chard leaves. Very young kale leaves would also work, and any other vegetables you have available such as peas or carrots.

5 tablespoons olive oil

1 onion, peeled and finely diced

1 carrot, diced (optional)

200g (7oz) shelled peas (optional)

1 celery stick, diced, or a handful of leaf celery, finely chopped

675g (1½lb) broad beans in the pod

350g (¾lb) fresh green leaves, ribs removed and cut into strips

1 tin of tomatoes

A sprig of thyme

A sprig of winter savory

2–4 cloves of garlic, chopped

Sea salt and freshly ground black pepper to taste

Heat the oil in a saucepan and add the chopped onions, herbs, garlic, celery, carrot and broad beans. Stir well and add a little water (not enough to cover the vegetables, but enough to give them something to cook in). Put a lid on the pan, turn down the heat and simmer the vegetables very slowly until the beans are tender. You want the flavours to come together and this can only happen if they are cooked slowly. Add more water if it looks as though everything is drying out too much.

Once the beans are tender add the tomatoes, peas and leaves. Cook until the tomato juice has evaporated a little and the leaves are wilted. Season with salt and lots of black pepper and serve with bread to mop it all up.

ORIENTAL GREENS

The spicier the green the less it needs to be cooked. Oriental mustard grown outside without protection will need no more than 50–60 seconds on a high heat. I drop the greens into boiling water before wringing them out and swishing them round a wok.

The Oriental greens meal I cook most often is wok-fried greens with angel hair, rice or soba noodles. The heat of the mustard stir-fried with the cool of pak choi and a bit of ginger is a classic. Groundnut oil is better for stir-fries than olive oil as it can be heated to a higher temperature without smoking or changing its flavour. Toasted sesame is a lovely oil, but should be added at the end of a dish, as you can't flash cook with it.

Wok-fried Oriental greens
A good glug of groundnut oil (about 2 tablespoons)

3 cloves of garlic, chopped

3 cups of Chinese chives, roughly chopped

A handful of Oriental greens (either mustard greens, mizuna, mibuna, pak choi or a mixture)

2 cups of mung or adzuki bean-sprouts

2 tablespoons soy or tamari sauce

2 teaspoons rice wine vinegar

1 small chilli, diced (optional)

Salt and pepper to taste

Add the oil to the wok and fry the garlic. Drop the Oriental greens into boiling water, drain and squeeze out any excess water. Dress with soy sauce and vinegar. Stir-fry the chives, sprouts and chillies with the garlic. Just as the chives begin to change colour, add the mustard and take it off the heat. Season with salt and pepper.

Serve with rice or noodles. You can pre-cook the noodles and add them to the wok at the last minute with the greens.

SUMMER

LAVENDER BISCUITS
I suppose the obvious thing to say here is that these are perfect for having with tea in the garden, but the truth is they're just as good anywhere.

Makes 10–12 biscuits:
150g (5oz) butter

90g (3½oz) caster sugar

225g (8oz) plain flour

1 egg yolk

1 tablespoon fresh lavender leaves, chopped

Roughly 1 teaspoon lavender flowers removed from the spike

Preheat the oven to 160°C (320°F) and grease two baking trays. Cream the butter and sugar together in a bowl until light

Lavender biscuits are delicious, light and perfect with afternoon tea.

and fluffy. Add the flour, egg yolk and lavender leaves and mix well. Turn the mixture onto a lightly floured surface and knead it into a smooth ball (this takes a little bit of elbow grease), then gently roll the ball into a cylinder shape about 8–10cm (3–4 in) in diameter. Cut the cylinder into 10–12 sections and press lavender flowers into the top of each biscuit. Bake in the oven for 15–18 minutes until the biscuits are firm, but not brown. Cool on trays for about 5 minutes (if you try to pick them up too soon they crumble) then move them to a wire rack to cool. You can keep the uncooked mixture in the fridge for several days.

CHLODNIK

This cold beetroot soup is traditionally made in the summer when cucumbers and radishes are also available.

5 small or 3 large beetroots with tops, flesh diced and leaves chopped
1 cucumber, roughly chopped
5 radishes, thinly sliced
1 large or 3 small bunching onions
½ lemon (or a bunch of sorrel)
3 teaspoon dill, chopped
1 teaspoon tarragon, chopped
450ml (¾ pint) natural yoghurt
50ml (2 fl oz) sour cream
Snipped chives, to garnish
2 eggs, hard-boiled and sliced, to garnish
Salt and pepper to taste

Tart blackcurrant sauce perfectly cuts through creamy yoghurt or ice-cream.

Cover the beetroots and leaves with water and cook until soft. Allow to cool. Combine the cucumber, radishes, bunching onions, lemon (or sorrel), dill and tarragon together in a bowl with the beetroot and blend together. The beetroot leaves will slightly muddy the colour, so if you want a very bright pink soup leave out the beetroot leaves. Season to taste and put in the fridge to cool. Once it's completely cool add the yoghurt and sour cream. Garnish with hard-boiled eggs and chives.

MY VERSION OF SALAD NIÇOISE
This is adapted from a recipe I found in a newspaper as a teenager.

A slug of olive oil

Red wine vinegar, to taste

1 large lettuce, washed and broken into pieces

5 radishes, sliced

2 shallots (or bunching onions), chopped

3 handfuls of small new potatoes (20–25 potatoes), washed – use salad types such as Ratte, Salad blue, Red Duke of York, Charlotte, Pink fir apple

8 nasturtium flowers

A small handful of calendula petals

A handful of French beans (if available), blanched

A handful of toasted walnuts

1 packet of feta cheese, crumbled

Salt and pepper, to taste

Boil the new potatoes and drain. Mix them with the finely chopped shallots (or bunching onions) and just enough olive oil to coat the mixture. Add red wine vinegar to taste. The potatoes will absorb the taste of the shallots and vinaigrette if they are warm. Once cool add the lettuce, radishes and beans if you have them and toss well. Add the walnuts and feta cheese and decorate with nasturtium flowers and calendula petals. Season to taste and add more vinaigrette if necessary.

RASPBERRY JAM ICE-CREAM
You can make this by siphoning off a little of the jam when you're making uncooked (or freezer) jam. To make the jam mix 1kg of fruit to 750g of caster sugar (or 3lb of raspberries to 2½lb of caster sugar), and stir together until the sugar dissolves. Leave it for half an hour and stir again. Do this three or four times until it begins to set, then store it in the freezer. If you stop before it gets thick you have wonderful coulis to pour over vanilla ice-cream.

BLACKCURRANT AND CHESTNUT ICE-CREAM SAUCE
Blackcurrant and chestnut purée is another fine addition to ice-cream. Rub 225g (just short of half a pound) of blackcurrants through a sieve or bash them up to release their juices. Blend 100g (about ¼lb) of chestnut purée with 50ml (2fl oz) of maple syrup or 50g (2oz) of brown sugar and slowly stir in the blackcurrant juice. Pour the sauce over vanilla ice-cream. You can omit the sugar altogether if you want a tart sauce.

AUTUMN

MINESTRONE SOUP

We eat a lot of this in early autumn, when you can still sit outside for lunch at the weekend with a hot, hearty soup. Yellow courgettes make it particularly colourful. This is a great recipe for using up a variety of vegetables that are just slightly past their prime, like those runner beans that have sat around unused for several days and the mountains of courgettes in the fridge.

Either use macaroni pasta (or similar) or rice. If you want the soup to be truly hearty add some white beans. As this soup cools it thickens a lot, so don't add too much rice or pasta.

---

3 tablespoons olive oil

1 large clove of garlic, chopped

1 onion, diced

1 tin of tomatoes or 3 large tomatoes, peeled, deseeded and diced

2 sticks of celery, diced (or a handful of leaf celery)

2 medium carrots, diced

2 courgettes, diced

2 large handfuls of green beans, sliced

2 medium boiling potatoes, diced

1.5 litres (2½ pints) stock or water

100g (4oz) Arborio rice or macaroni-style pasta

1 tin of cannellini beans or a handful of fresh shelling beans

2 tablespoons chopped parsley, 1–2 leaves of sage and a sprig of rosemary

For a summer taste add a bunch of chopped basil leaves

Fresh Parmesan for the table

Salt and pepper, to taste

My garden in a soup. Borscht garnished with chop suey petals, chives and dollop of crème fraîche.

In a large soup pot, sauté the onions and garlic in olive oil so that the onions turn translucent and the garlic just begins to colour. Add the vegetables, a little salt to taste and stir well, gently softening the vegetables. After about 5 minutes add the water or stock and bring to the boil. Gently simmer until the vegetables are almost done, but still firm. This takes about 45–60 minutes.

Add the rice or pasta, beans, parsley, sage, rosemary and half the basil if you're using it. Cook for about ten minutes, stirring constantly until the rice is just cooked (it will continue to cook as the soup cools). Ladle out the soup and serve with fresh basil and Parmesan.

BORSCHT BEETROOT SOUP

There are many ways to make borscht. My mother learnt to make her version from some 'White Russians' in Hong Kong. Her recipe is puréed with lots of cabbage.

In the summer my recipe is based on my friend Helenka's version, substituting lemon for vinegar and using fresh peas and baby beetroot leaves. By autumn I want more nascent flavours and am back to using vinegar and even a little chilli to give a sharp, yet earthy flavour.

Borscht is one of those soups that improves with age. Cook big batches and enjoy it again the next day, or ladle it into sealed containers and pop it in the freezer, as it keeps very well this way.

5–6 medium-sized beetroot, washed, peeled and coarsely grated

4 tablespoons olive oil or a mixture of half oil, half butter

A good slug of white wine vinegar (flavoured with tarragon is best)

2 large carrots, thinly sliced

2 leeks (if available), thinly sliced

2–3 onions, chopped

2 large potatoes, washed, peeled and diced

2 tablespoons chopped parsley, perhaps with a little tarragon if you don't have flavoured vinegar

2 bay leaves

1 small chilli, deseeded and sliced

1.5 litres (2½ pints) water or beef stock

Crème frâiche, to garnish

Salt and pepper, to taste

Snipped chives and chop suey flowers, to garnish

Keeping a quarter of the grated beetroot aside, put the rest in a bowl and splash on some vinegar. This is very much a taste thing, but I wouldn't have the beetroot floating in vinegar. Set aside for about an hour. Braise the onions, leeks and carrots with the parsley (and tarragon, if using) in oil on a low heat for about 10 minutes, or until the onions start to brown. Drain the beetroots and add with the potatoes to the vegetables. Add a little salt, the bay leaves, water or stock and let the mix cook for at least an hour, simmering on a low heat. Add the remaining uncooked beetroot and taste, you may want a little more vinegar. At this point I add the chilli and season. Serve with a big dollop of crème frâiche and garnish with chives and petals.

Courgette cake is a vehicle for courgette glut. It's a very basic cake recipe for you to adapt whichever way you want.

My mother blends the whole soup and substitutes the raw beetroot for shredded cabbage. You can also strain the soup towards the end so that you have a clear broth in which you can float mushroom tortellini – filled pasta dumplings.

COURGETTE CAKE

This is my mother's recipe. It's basically a banana bread recipe converted for excess courgettes. From the basic recipe you can go any way you want – add dried fruit, nuts, dates, dark chocolate chips, exchange the sugar for honey (though use slightly less or it'll be too wet) or go wild and use part wholemeal flour and part white, seaweed (dulse) and a little chilli powder.

1 medium courgette or 2 small ones, topped, tailed and shredded – it's best to leave them for a day so that they lose a bit of their moisture

100g (4oz) softened butter

150g (5oz) soft brown sugar

2 eggs

200g (7oz) flour

3 teaspoons baking powder

Beat the butter and sugar together until light and fluffy. Add the eggs, one at a time, and beat as hard as you can. Add the flour and baking powder. Mix together, then add the courgettes.

I cook it in a bread tin because I like the utilitarian look of cake made this way. Pre-grease whatever tin you use and cook

a pancake mixture with egg whites and as long as you own a whisk you'll be able to make it.

450g (1lb) Jerusalem artichokes, scrubbed, peeled and diced

110g (4oz) Stilton cheese, cut into cubes

110g (4oz) double cream

1 heaped tablespoon plain flour

2 eggs + 2 egg whites (use the leftover egg yolks to make shortbread biscuits)

28g (1oz) melted butter

salt, pepper and nutmeg, to taste

You'll need a large and fairly deep ovenproof dish to bake the soufflé in, as it will rise up the edge of the dish as it cooks. Preheat the oven to 200°C (400°F).

Boil the artichokes, drain them and then purée them in a liquidizer (or pass them through a sieve). Add the cream, flour, eggs (not the egg whites), butter and seasoning and blitz again. Pour the resulting batter into a large bowl. Whisk the egg whites until they are stiff and fold them into the batter. Add the Stilton and pour into the ovenproof dish. A soufflé will rise considerably, the dish will need at least 10–15cm (4–6 in) headroom between the batter and the top.

Bake for 25–30 minutes, keeping an eye on it, and serve immediately. Some people like the centre runny, some like it stiffer, it's a matter of taste. Serve with crusty bread to mop up, and my mother says it should also be served with 'some sort of neat and tidy green side dish', which I think means spinach or similar seasonal greens.

for about 40–45 minutes at 180°C (350°F) for a normal oven, or 160°C (350°F) for a fan oven. You can also make them into cupcakes, cooked for about 10–12 minutes, but keep an eye on them.

When the cake is cooked, a skewer or knife inserted into the centre should come out clean. Remove and cool on a wire tray. It's very good sliced with butter.

WINTER

MY MOTHER'S JERUSALEM ARTICHOKE SOUFFLÉ

This is so good that guests often go home with a bag of Jerusalem artichokes and instructions (on both how to grow the vegetables and how to bake the soufflé). Don't be put off by the soufflé bit, it's just

JERUSALEM ARTICHOKE GRATIN

This is made in much the same way as you would a potato dauphinoise.

1kg (2lb) Jerusalem artichokes
A slug of olive oil
2 cloves of garlic, chopped
Salt and pepper, to taste
1 large tub of single cream or a mixture of cream and milk
28g (1oz) butter
At least 50g (2oz) Parmesan
Breadcrumbs and nutmeg (optional)

Cook the artichokes in water for about 6 minutes (if they are fresh from the ground they can cook very quickly, so keep an eye on them). They should not be fully cooked. Drain, cool, peel and slice. In a shallow, ovenproof dish place a third of your artichokes and scatter a little chopped garlic and oil over the top. Season the layer with salt and pepper. Create another two or three layers (until you reach near the top of the dish), repeating the garlic, oil, salt and pepper.

Heat some single cream (or cream and milk) and pour it over the artichokes. Dot some cubes of butter over the top and sprinkle over a generous amount of Parmesan or similar hard cheese, you want the cheese to melt through the artichokes. I like to add breadcrumbs as well (first coated in oil) and perhaps a little nutmeg. Bake in the oven for about 45 minutes at 180° C (350°F) for a normal oven or 160°C (320°F) for a fan oven.

COURGETTE WITH PECORINO CHEESE AND BASIL ON PASTA

Frozen, grated courgette is useful for bulking up soups and tomato-based pasta sauces, and also works particularly well in frittatas. This recipe can be made with either fresh basil and courgettes or frozen supplies. If you are making it with fresh, don't cook the basil, and stir in all the cheese at the same time. You don't need to defrost the courgettes or basil.

450g (1lb) shredded courgettes
2 tablespoons olive oil
1–2 cloves of garlic, finely chopped or minced (if you mince garlic it tastes a lot stronger)
2 heaped tablespoons Pecorino Romano cheese (or substitute Parmesan or any other hard yellow cheese)
2 cubes of frozen basil (or about 10 leaves of fresh basil)
3 tablespoons crème fraîche (optional)
Salt and freshly ground pepper, to taste

Sauté the frozen courgettes in oil on a high heat until they are golden, constantly moving them about. This should take no more than 4 minutes. Turn down the heat, add the garlic and salt and pepper to taste. Cook until the courgettes are tender, but retain a little crispness. Add a tablespoon of the cheese and stir in along with the basil until everything has melted. If the mixture looks a little too thick add a couple of tablespoons of cooked pasta water or add crème fraîche for a richer dish.

Toss the mixture over cooked and drained short pasta (orzo pasta is good) and add the remaining grated cheese. Serve at room temperature, or it's surprisingly good cold.

I am the perfect housewife: Poppyseed rolls!

CHARD, GARLIC AND HOT PEPPER WITH INSTANT NOODLES

This is the ultimate trashy fast food, made good through homegrown greens.

One packet instant noodles
A big handful of chard leaves, about 450g (1lb)
4 tablespoons olive oil
3 or 4 small cloves of garlic, peeled and chopped
½ teaspoon chilli pepper, finely chopped
Salt, to taste
Lemon wedges, to serve

Wash the chard and remove the stems from the leaves. Chop the stems and leaves into strips. In a large pan gently sauté the stems with the oil, garlic and chilli until they are firm, but beginning to go tender, then add the leaves and sprinkle on a little salt. It takes no more than 10 minutes for the chard to be tender and the garlic golden. Cook the instant noodles and add to the pan with a tablespoon or two of the cooking water and mingle. Serve with lemon wedges.

BITTER GREENS

Bitter greens are served all over Italy in local trattorias just after the main meal to help digestion. They're particularly good with sausages, pork and other hearty meats. You can mix and match your greens to what's available over winter. The more mustard and rocket you include, the more bitter the taste.

1 bunch of Swiss chard
1 bunch of mustard greens
1 bunch of spinach or young kale leaves
1 bunch of rocket
2 cloves of garlic, finely chopped
3 tablespoons olive oil
Salt, to taste
Lemon wedges, to serve

Wash the greens well and then wilt them in a saucepan. It's best to wilt each green separately as they will cook at slightly different times. Remove any tough midribs and sauté the chard first as this will take longest – you may need to add a tablespoon or so of water. Add salt to taste. Next cook the mustard fast if you don't want too bitter a taste. Then spinach, then rocket.

Put all the wilted greens together and sauté in a large pan with olive oil and garlic. The garlic is not supposed to be fried, just warmed amongst the greens. Season to taste and serve with lemon wedges.

EDIBLE SEEDS

Buckwheat is a lovely seed, triangular in shape with a very tough husk. One way to deal with the husk is to sprout the seed before baking.

Caraway is a biennial so you have to wait until the second year to get any seed. Use the seed in sourdoughs. The seed stores for about a year in an airtight container out of direct sunlight. The leaves can be used in soups and salads.

Dill seed and leaves are good for baking, particularly in sourdough breads.

Fennel seed is lovely in a wholemeal bread.

Himalayan balsam, *Impatiens glandulifera,* is an out-of-control alien or a great source of nectar for bees, depending on who you speak to. One way to control their slightly rampant nature is to collect the seed. This is easier said than done as it has a spring mechanism that shoots them out when ripe. It seems easiest to put a whole bag over the entire flowerhead and shake.

Lavender seeds take pastries to a new level. Use fresh seeds in shortbreads, biscuits or sweet bread.

Lovage is a very tall herb, growing to 2m (6 ft) tall. The seed can be used in baking and is said to be good for detoxification, but lovage is not ideal for a small garden.

Love-in-a-mist, *Nigella damascena,* **seeds** are similar but not quite as tasty as the black cumin, *Nigella sativa,* prettier though.

Opium poppy, *Papaver somniferum,* **Corn poppy,** *Papaver rhoea,* **Arctic poppy,** *Papaver nudicaule* and all their resulting cultivars.

Pumpkins – look out for semi-huskless varieties like 'Baby Bear', or roast ones with husks on a baking tray. I experimented with several different flavours last year and found that honey, soy sauce, chilli, sea salt, and cracked black pepper are all ideal. Mix the pumpkins with enough olive oil and your desired ingredients to coat the seeds

Phormium seeds are edible and slightly spicy. Allow the seedheads to dry completely before collecting the seed. They are best used in baking.

and roast at 120–150°C (250–300°F). You have to keep a constant eye on them to make sure they don't burn and eat them quickly as they'll melt into a gooey mess. They make a great bonfire night treat with a good bitter beer.

Sunflowers usually contain lots of seeds, but trying to remove a sunflower seed from its husk is tough. The easiest way is to roast the seed for 30–40 minutes at 120–150°C (250–300°F) on a baking tray. Add a little salt if you want; the best way to eat them is to chew and spit. If you're patient you can remove them from their hulls, but as you have to bash the hull the seed tends to come out mushed. You can cream this using a food processor (or by hand with a rolling pin in a bowl) to make sunflower butter. It's a laborious process, but the results are delicious.

FERMENTED THINGS

WILD FERMENTATION

Wild fermentation is about harnessing the good yeast that surrounds us and using it to ferment food into a nutritious state. These are tangy, bubbling, intense foods that take a little getting used to if you've never tried them. The process is ancient and on the whole relies more on instinct and taste than precise instruction. It requires very little energy, just some sunrays or a little indoor heat and you're away. Unlike most other forms of processing food, this is a truly off-the-grid way to store your food.

All sorts of different factors figure in how long it takes to ferment a vegetable or make a sourdough yeast. The bible for this culture is *Wild Fermentation* by Sandor Katz. I started off rather innocently learning how to make sauerkraut from Daphne Lambert, one of the Soil Sisters, and now have bubbling crocks of ginger beer, whey ferments, soured beets and various other projects littering my worktops.

SAUERKRAUT
This recipe is from Daphne Lambert.

This kraut will blow any shop-bought, manufactured stuff out of the scene. For a start it remains crunchy.

Choose two, firm white or red cabbages (if you are buying from a Farmers' Market choose the freshest you can find as moisture content is important). Any cabbage will work, but look for the compact, round-headed versions to start with as these are the easiest to work with. Red cabbage will create pink kraut.

Chop the cabbage in half and remove the heart, then finely chop the rest.

In a sturdy bowl pound the cabbage with a rolling pin for about 10 minutes. Slowly the cabbage will start to glisten and by the end you should be able to squeeze moisture out by the handful. Put a thin layer (a teaspoon or so) of salt over the area of cabbage that will be exposed to air, cover the bowl loosely with a tea towel and leave overnight. The following morning you should find moisture or even a small amount of liquid at the bottom of the bowl.

You'll need a large Kilner jar, Mason jar or ceramic crock with a lid for the next part. Place about 5–10cm (2–4 in) of cabbage

Gundru is traditionally made using Swiss chard, but you can also make it with mustards and kales.

at the bottom of the jar and layer with salt (a teaspoon or less) or seaweed (dulse is a good low-salt alternative). You can also layer other vegetables, such as chopped up Swiss chard or kale, and add spices, such as caraway seed. Next you need to pound this layer down to exclude air. This is very important. If you were just to leave the veggies exposed to air they would rot, but by excluding air and adding salt you create conditions that invite the good bacteria into the fermentation process.

Keep layering, salting and pounding until you reach the top of the jar. At the top of the jar add another layer of salt. By the top

enough moisture should have come out that you can see the brine appear. If there is no brine (it can take time to appear as the salt draws out the moisture) top up with a brine solution of 1 tablespoon of salt to 250ml (½ pint) of water.

You will need to keep the cabbage weighed down in the brine. The simplest way to do this is to place a glass or jam jar full of water in the mouth of the jar to weigh down the contents. The kraut will take anything from five days to over a week to ferment. You may see a scum appear at the top, this is no bad thing, just skim it off. Once the kraut tastes tangy it's ready, you don't want it to go soft. When it's suitably tangy, put the lid on and store in the fridge or cool conditions. If the brine levels go down, top them up as the brine keeps the kraut preserved. You can preserve the kraut by heat processing, but I think the more sensible way is just to make it and eat it, and when one batch is over start up another lot. It's alive, enjoy it that way.

GUNDRU

This method is taken from Sandor Katz's *Wild Fermentation*.

This is a Nepalese method of fermenting chard or brassica leaves in their own juices. It is very simple, rewardingly so. It has a strong earthy flavour and a very sour end note. I think it's a little addictive. It's easiest to make with Swiss chard leaves, once you've made one successful batch, try kales.

Pick as much chard as you can. It's hard to be precise, but two handfuls is a good starting point. Leave them to wilt in the sun for a day. If you don't have any sun then you could use the bottom of your oven on its lowest heat setting.

Once wilted, pound the leaves with a rolling pin in a sturdy container. You are going to pound and pound until you start to see juices appearing. Do this in layers,

Opposite: A fermented gundru leaf.
Below: Wilt the leaves in the sun for a day before packing in jars.

pounding and pushing with your fingers until you have packed as much in as possible. Two handfuls will fit into a jam jar so that should give you an idea how much pounding needs to be done. Once you have pushed all the leaves in you should have a fair amount of liquid. This will smell very intensely of the greens you've pounded. Replace the lid and put the jar somewhere warm and sunny. It will need two to three weeks in the sun or somewhere warm, about 24–27°C (75–80°F). The flavour will intensify to become quite sour. It's a taste thing, the longer you leave it the more sour it becomes. You can either enjoy it raw or air dry it and use it like seaweed, in which case it needs to be perfectly dry, but will keep indefinitely. Use it in soups and stews where it will add a slightly sour note (it's good in borscht).

Brews

HERBAL TEAS

Even the most organically sourced, ethically-traded herbal tea contains packaging and transport costs. We seem obsessed with travelling half way across the world to find some wonder herb to save us from colds or to wake us up when the same local remedy could be growing in our own back garden. Rosemary tea doesn't sound as exciting as the zing of hibiscus, but it's just as good as a pick-me-up and it can grow outside your back door all year round.

It does take quite an effort to supply yourself with herb teas all year, but start by just growing some summer teas and see how you get on. Then you can start to harvest and store for winter.

Mint is the easiest to get going with, all you need is reasonable soil or a bag of compost and a pot or two. In their natural habit (or in the ground) mints like to run all over the place, so life in a pot is a little restrictive, but for mint that's a good thing or your garden can quickly get overrun. Each year by midspring you need to re-pot your mints to keep them healthy, just turf them out and shake them up a bit, teasing out the roots so you can discard the older middle section and re-pot the whitest youngest roots in fresh compost.

The plant will quickly respond with new, lush growth that makes the best tea. If you want to grow mint in the ground but are afraid of it invading your space, grow it in larger plastic pots with the bottoms cut off to restrict the roots.

HOW TO MAKE HERBAL TEA

As a rule you need three teaspoons of fresh herbs per cup. Fresh teas from your garden are a truly different experience from dried, commercial ones. The flavours deepen with steeping, so you'll want to experiment to find your own preference. I think tea tastes better if it's made in a pot. With most teas you can get a second steeping or you can just add more leaves to the pot. Young leaves tend to taste best, and as a plant begins to flower you often lose some of the potency as energy is diverted to flowering.

Rosemary and lemon balm grow wild in my park, a throwback to when it was a Victorian garden. It's worth keeping your eyes out for these wild cultivated finds.

Lemon balm is ideal for upset stomachs and hangovers.

HARVESTING, STORING AND DRYING TEAS

Collect young, healthy material to dry before it starts to flower. Midsummer is your best bet, but every year I seem to miss the mark and end up drying at the end of summer. My teas still taste good, so I'm not worrying too much about it.

Sage, thyme, rosemary and winter savory are around all year so I don't worry about drying them. Plus I only drink these when I have a cold. But mint, verbena, lemon verbena, lemon balm, rosehip and oswego are gone come mid-autumn. I dry most of my herbs either hanging upside down over a radiator or in old cotton sheets hung up a little like hammocks in a warm room out of direct sunlight (not in your bathroom, it's too humid). An airing cupboard or spare room is ideal. I do hang some mints upside down in the kitchen, but if you cook a lot of smelly foods then your mint absorbs this. I can well see that a dehydrator makes the best job of this, but air-drying works in most cases. It is possible to dry herbs in a very low oven at 45–55°C (110–130°F) but it's also very easy to overdry them to a useless flavourless crisp this way.

Your leaves are ready for storage once they are dry and very slightly crispy to touch. Strip them from their stems and store them in airtight containers out of direct sunlight.

HERB TEAS

All of the ingredients for the teas below, apart from raspberry and rose, are as happy grown in a pot as they are in soil, and raspberry leaves can be sourced out foraging. Lemon grass actively prefers a pot. Olive, rosemary, lemon verbena, thyme, winter savory, sage, lemon grass and lavender will cope with full sun and very baked conditions and can deal with exposed sites as long as they are warm. The rest are happier with part of the day in shade, particularly if they are in a pot.

Bronze fennel makes a beautiful tea. I prefer the taste of the leaves over the seed heads – I reserve these for baking and cooking. Fennel is good for indigestion and delicious with a little honey.

Echinacea, the flower cones have antiviral and antibacterial properties, it doesn't taste of much so mix it in something more exciting, such as lemon verbena.

Feverfew, a few leaves at the beginning of a migraine and you can sometimes stop it in its tracks. Good for generally calming sore heads.

Lavender flowers, fresh or dried, give a distinctly floral note. Good with black teas or to lift strong-tasting herbs like rosemary.

Lemon balm, good for soothing sore stomachs and particularly good after a night's drinking. It's very gentle and only mildly lemony in flavour. I think it's best combined with lemon verbena.

Lemon basil tastes better than you might imagine – hot.

SOME TEA COMBINATIONS

Stevia with everything for sweetness.

Lemon balm and fresh ginger.

Dried or fresh orange peel and lemon verbena.

Fennel and rosemary as a pick-me-up.

Thyme and sage, or rosemary and sage and (as long as you're not seeing anyone) garlic make great remedies for colds, add honey if necessary

Hyssop and thyme is another combination for coughs, add plenty of honey to make it palatable.

Lemon grass is very easy to grow, but tender and will need to be brought inside for the winter.

Lemon verbena is my all-time favourite. Think of lemon boiled sweets in a cup. It doesn't like wet, cold winters so put it somewhere sheltered for the winter and be prepared to fleece if necessary.

Linden flowers, lime tree flowers should be picked just as the flowers open. They taste of vanilla and are truly worth the effort of picking (they're small and need drying on a rack).

Mints. The following mints make good teas. Experiment by blending different mints together.

Ginger mint *Mentha* x *gracilis*.

Eastern mint *M. longifolia* subsp. *schimperi*.

Peppermint *M.* x *piperita*.

Longee's mint *M.* x *piperita* 'Longee's'.

Garden mint *M. sativa*.

Spearmint *M. spicata* – can taste a little like mouthwash if used on its own.

Moroccan mint *M. spicata* var. *crispa* 'Moroccan'.

Swiss mint *M. spicata* 'Swiss'.

Yerba Buena Satureja Douglassi has a clean mint flavour (also very good in mojitos). It is not fully hardy and will need to come inside over winter.

Oswego *Monarda didyma* tea is delicious and tastes somewhere between peppermint and sage. The leaves can be dried for winter use.

Olive leaves, say four or five, gently boiled so that the water goes an amber colour seems to stop a cold in its tracks.

Pot marigold flowers *Calendula officinalis*, preferably dried, make a lovely looking addition to teas.

Raspberry leaf is good for mouth inflammations or sores. It's lovely-tasting and can also be used as a preparation for childbirth. The young leaves are best by midsummer, so start drying for autumn and winter use.

Roman chamomile *Chamaemelum nobile*, sends me into a laid-back stupor in seconds. Not one for all-nighters. Harvest the flowers in summer and dry them on racks out of direct light.

Damson vodka: how to make friends and influence people.

Rosehips should be picked and air-dried on a rack. An excellent source of vitamin C, they need to be gently boiled for several minutes to release their sharp, slightly sweet flavour. Rosehips are particularly good when combined with black tea and honey.

Rosemary is antifungal and good for sore throats.

Sage is antifungal and good for colds and sore throats.

Stevia is incredibly sweet, you only need one leaf per cup, it is also tender and will need to come in for the winter.

Common thyme is a powerful antiseptic. It should not be used if pregnant and some people find it irritating to the throat so use in small doses.

Lemon thyme, *Thymus x citriodorus,* is tastier and less irritating than other thymes.

Winter Savory, *Satureja montana,* has a spicy flavour and is good for sore throats. Do not take it if you are pregnant.

Note: If you are pregnant seek advice before brewing your own herbal teas as some herbs, such as hyssop, should not be consumed during pregnancy or while breast-feeding.

FRUIT LIQUEURS AND COCKTAILS

SPICED CRAB APPLE VODKA

I've based this around pickled crab apples, but changed the vinegar for vodka to make a more useful solution!

1.5kg (3lb) crab apples
1 cinnamon stick
450g (1lb) caster sugar
1 very small piece of mace
5 cloves
1 vanilla pod
1 litre (1¾ pints) vodka

Stuff the crab apples into a large glass jar with the spices and sugar, then cover them completely with vodka and leave them for two months. Once the vodka has gone a golden colour, strain it to drink and use the pickled crab apples for dessert. They're particularly good with thick cream and sugar.

BLACKBERRY WHISKY

This is an alternative to the popular sloe gin. If you don't like whisky you could try vodka, but I've found even adamant non-whisky drinkers like it.

There is no point buying the expensive stuff as you're adding a lot of sugar, but don't go too cheap or the whisky will be watery.

For a litre (1¾ pints) of whisky you need 550g (1¼lb) of blackberries and 275g (10oz) of raw cane sugar. You'll need some sort of lidded container to store the blackberries and whisky in – a large Kilner jar is perfect. You could just put the blackberries and sugar in the whisky bottle, but you'll have to drink quite a bit of the whisky first!

Mix all the ingredients together and shake until all the sugar is dissolved (harder work than you think, the more hands the better). You'll need to keep shaking the mixture every day for the next two weeks to stop the sugar from settling at the bottom of the jar. If your container isn't watertight then you can just rest the bottle on its side (against a tea towel) and keep turning it every day. After two weeks you just need to shake or turn the bottle once a week. By week eight it's ready to drink. I think it looks best if you decant it back into its original bottle, straining out the fruit. The fruit can be used to make a boozy compote that's excellent over vanilla ice-cream.

DAMSON VODKA

Made in exactly the same way as blackberry whisky. However, because the damsons won't break down as quickly as the blackberries it will take about three months to make. You need to prick the damsons (a tooth pick works best) before you put them in the vodka. Try and only use ripe damsons.

SLOE GIN

Sloe gin is also made using the same method. The sloes need pricking, like damsons, and old-timers always say that they taste best after a hard frost has softened them. Alternatively, you can pick the fruit and put it in the freezer overnight before you use it.

The last three drinks on this page are very sweet and the resulting liqueur is very syrupy and tends to be drunk in small amounts. The less sugar you use the drier the taste, particularly damson and sloe gin or vodka.

SLOE GIN FIZZ

I adapted this cocktail recipe from one in a pamphlet I found inside a 1950s ice crusher called *The Smart Hostess/The Discriminating Host*.

A shot of sloe gin or damson vodka

Half a shot of lemon juice

½ teaspoon sugar syrup (made by dissolving equal parts sugar and water in a pan over a low heat until you have a syrup), cooled

Soda water

Shake the gin (or vodka), lemon juice and sugar syrup together well and add soda water to make a long drink.

Spiced crab apple vodka is actually the thing I am most proud of making.

CHILLI VODKA

750ml (1½ pint) bottle of vodka

3 chillies, preferably one orange habenero, one red bird pepper, and one green jalapeno

De-seed and slice the chillies into short lengths then put them into the bottle of vodka. Stand the vodka somewhere out of direct sunlight, at room temperature, and shake once a day for two days. Taste, if it's not hot enough let it sit for another two days, but I'd advise no longer as it can quickly become bitter. Strain the vodka back into its original bottle. This is wonderful in Bloody Mary or just on its own for cold winter nights.

RESOURCES

CHICKENS

My lovely chickens Gertrude and Alice B. (coop and all) came from **www.poultrypark.com**

www.backyardchickens.com has a wealth of information on how to keep hens happy and some crazy chicken coop designs.

PICKLING AND FERMENTING

Meeting the **SOIL SISTERS**, Miche Fabre Lewin and Daphne Lambert, has been a life-changing experience. Their cooking is how good homegrown food should really be treated. Miche and Daphne offer courses on nutrition, seasonal eating and green cuisine. They also make incredible cocktails called Rainbow Spirits. *greencuisine.penrhos.com/ events/soil_sisters.html*

FOREST GARDENING

MARTIN CRAWFORD'S FOREST GARDEN website offers courses, mail-order nursery and links. It's hard to describe just how magical Martin's garden is, it's a little like a natural sweet shop. Everywhere you look is something interesting to pick and eat. *www.agroforestry.co.uk*

WILLOW WEAVING

If you want to make some beautiful supports for your plants, **SALLY** is a leading organic gardener and a dab hand at whipping a bit of willow or bramble into something magnificent. Sally offers courses in willow weaving. *www.gardenorganic.org.uk/ events/courses*

SEEDS
GROWING OLD

For a lovely mix of heritage seed, some perennial edibles like tree onions and varieties that grandma grew. These beautifully packaged seeds make excellent presents. *www.pennardplants.com*

HERITAGE SEED LIBRARY

You have to become a member of this seed library that specializes in local and heritage seeds from around Europe that are not commercially available. The membership entitles you to six varieties a year and encourages seed saving. *www.gardenorganic.org.uk/hsl/ index.php*

FRANCHI SEEDS

Italian seed company specializing in local and heritage seeds, particularly good for cut-and-come-again salads and raddichios. Nice catalogue, often with good recipes. *www.seedsofitaly.com*

REAL SEED COMPANY

These really are the best in rare, unusual and heritage seeds for the kitchen garden. All their seed is open-pollinated and produced on small farms, trialled in Wales for hardiness, and they come with instructions on how to save them so you don't have to buy next year. *www.realseeds.co.uk*

CHASE SEEDS / THE ORGANIC GARDENING CATALOGUE

One-stop shop for all your organic gardening needs from books, to seeds and seaweed fertilizers. Lovely wildflower mixes. *www.organiccatalog.com*

SUFFOLK HERBS

Unusual vegetables, herbs and flower seed. One of the first companies to stock Oriental vegetable seeds. *www.suffolkherbs.com*

Suffolk Herbs are now part of **KINGS SEEDS**, they have a very extensive vegetable list. *www.kingsseeds.com*

CHILTERNS SEED

Amazingly long list of flowers, trees, shrubs, herbs and vegetables with brilliant descriptions. There are some real finds in this catalogue. *www.chilternseeds.co.uk*

NICKY'S SEED

A good vegetable sowing chart as well as interesting and unusual vegetables. Some, including chillies, are offered in sensible, smaller-size packets. *www.nickys-nursery.co.uk*

DOBIES

Extensive list includes young vegetable plants, mushroom spores, seed potatoes and some interesting mustards. *www.dobies.co.uk*

MAIL-ORDER NURSERIES
EDULIS

Fantastic nursery and design business with permaculture leanings. The nursery sells a wide range of very unusual, edible ornamentals. *www.edulis.co.uk*

JEKKA'S HERB FARM

Award-winning grower specializing in organic herbs for medicinal and culinary uses. Sells mail-order plants and seeds. It's the only place I can find Cuban oregano. *www.jekkasherbfarm.com*

PRACTICAL

THE ROYAL HORTICULTURAL SOCIETY is still the biggest and best at doling out information on exactly how to do a gardening task. The 'Grow Your Own' section of their website is particularly well laid out and useful.
www.rhs.org.uk/growyourown/

THE US NATIONAL CENTER FOR HOME FOOD PRESERVATION provides the definitive guide to preserving everything safely.
www.uga.edu/nchfp/

PLANTS FOR A FUTURE
Amazing resource of edible, medicinal and useful plants. Very good section on edible flowers.
www.pfaf.org

VIDEO GOOGLE
A huge resource for finding films. Good for baking and gardening techniques.
www.video.google.com/

INSPIRATIONAL

THE PERMACULTURE ASSOCIATION has a good selection of short films discussing the ideas behind permaculture and transition towns.
www.permaculture.tv
www.permaculture.org.uk

GROFUN
G.ro.f.u.n was started by Nadia Hillman in Bristol and aims to get as many people as possible growing their own food. They run a community exchange scheme, swapping and coordinating with neighbours to grow food cooperatively.
www.grofun.org.uk

INCREDIBLE EDIBLE TODMORDEN
This is one town's adventure in growing more food. The town aims to be sustainable in vegetables by 2018. From guerilla composting to the 'Egg Map' showing surplus eggs, there's plenty of information on how to do the growing thing as a community.
www.incredible-edible-todmorden.co.uk

CITY FARMER
City farming news from around the world.
www.cityfarmer.info

URBAN HOMESTEAD ADVICE
How-to homestead provides unique video how-to's on homesteading outside the rural sphere.
www.howtohomestead.org

COMMON GROUND
The home of Apple Day, community orchards and celebrating the local.
www.commonground.org.uk

FEDERATION OF COMMUNITY GARDENS AND CITY FARMS
The hub of British urban farming.
www.farmgarden.org.uk

PICK-YOUR-OWN FARMS
Look for your local farms, as well as finding preserving tips, equipment and jars
www.pickyourownfarms.org.uk

EDIBLE ESTATES HOME
LA-based artist Fritz Haeg initiated the Edible Estates project that proposed the replacement of the domestic front lawn in the US with highly productive edible landscapes.
www.farmgarden.org.uk

FURTHER READING

Sue Stickland, *Backyard Seed Saving* (Eco-logic books)

Dominique Guillet, *The Seeds of Kokopelli – A Manual for the Production of Seed in the Family Garden* (Association Kokopelli www.kokopelli.asso.fr)

Martin Crawford, *Creating a Forest Garden – Perennial Crops for a Changing Climate* (Green Books)

Patrick Whitefield, *The Earth Care Manual* (Permanent Publications)

Patrick Whitefield, *How to make a forest garden* (Permanent Publications)

Joy Larkcom, *Creative Vegetable Gardening* (Mitchell Beazley)
Joy Larkcom, *Grow Your Own* (Frances Lincoln)

Joy Larkcom, *Oriental Vegetables – The Complete Guide for the Gardening Cook* (Kodansha International)
Barbara Kingsolver, Camille Kingsolver and Steven L. Hopp, *Animal, Vegetable, Miracle – A Year of Food Life* (Harper Collins)

Masanobu Fukuoka, *The One-Straw Revolution* (Frances Lincoln)

FORAGING

Miles Irving, *The Forager Handbook – A guide to the Edible Plants of Britain* (Ebury Press)

Richard Mabey, *Food for Free* (Collins)

ACKNOWLEDGEMENTS

This is the year that I truly found my garden, and to have that captured by two people whose work I love has been an immense privilege. So to Simon Wheeler and Juliet Glaves, thank you for your lovely images.

To those who sit at my table, thank you to Clare Savage, Emily Castles, Deborah Adams, Dave Paine, Syd and Beth, Jeremy and Ingrid, Sue and Les. We loved our bell tent at Green Man, almost as much as we loved swimming in the Usk.

To lovely Charlie who is much more than an editor, thank you for so patiently weaving this one together. Your cutflower tales were a soothing balm when stuck at this computer.

To my lovely family and in particular to my mum who taught me to cook, garden and bang things together, in short, how to make the world around me.

To the crew behind the series, Andy Payne and Geraint Lewis, Geraint Evans and Nat Reid, Gary Hawkey and Paul Scurrell and Super8 Neil, thank you for not stepping on the flowers!

To the man few will notice and even less see, Keith Brown.

To Caroline and Lorna at Ebury, thank you for your patience.

To Kyle for letting go.

To Borra, Jan and Emma for sorting it all out.

To the many people who make Kings Heath such a cool place to live in, in particular Kings Heath Library, those who joined Grofun, and the Clean and Green Committee.

And to my husband for his lovely illustrations, for putting up with all my experimental recipes, for feeding the chickens and loving the dog.

INDEX

A

amaranth 56, 122–3, 179
anemone 170
angelica 66, 179
aphids 45, 76, 130
apple 19, 25, 116, 133, 144, 151, 153–6
　　and blackberry jam 203
　　design ideas 62, 65
　　harvest 196, 198
　　rings 212
asparagus 133, 136, 138–9, 144
aster 168, 180
aubergine 24, 40, 48, 51

B

baby veg 80, 83
basil 31, 51, 146–7, 151, 214, 231–3, 246
bay 147, 183

beans 9, 43, 51, 60, 67, 75–9, 192, 214, 226
　　see also specific species
beetroot 51, 56, 66, 80–3, 188, 214, 223–5
　　soup 226–8
biodiversity 10, 188–91
birds 103, 162
biscuits, lavender 222–3
bitter greens 233
blackberry 26, 29, 153, 154, 160, 196, 214
　　and apple jam 203
　　whisky 247
blackcurrant 160–2, 196
　　and chestnut ice-cream sauce 225
blackfly 76
blanching 212–14
blossom end rot 118
blueberry 151, 153, 162–3
borscht 226–8

bouquets 181–3
boysenberry 160
brassicas 41, 51, 92–3, 176, 192, 238
　　see also specific species
broad bean 51, 75–6, 146, 221
broccoli 51, 56, 133, 141, 191, 214
　　purple sprouting 65, 168–9, 179
Brussels sprouts 46, 66, 67, 83, 89
buckwheat 43–5, 191, 234
bulbs 169–70

C

cabbage 19, 25, 45, 51, 56, 89, 191–2, 236–8
cake, courgette 228
caraway 234
carrot 23, 32, 51, 54, 83–4, 168, 179, 191, 214, 221, 226, 228

carrot fly 83, 84
caterpillars 88
cauliflower 51, 56, 89
celery 51, 84, 221, 226
chamomile 243
chard 31, 67, 238
   garlic and hot pepper with
     instant noodles 233
   rainbow 31
   red 31
   see also Swiss chard
cherry 154, 196
chestnut and blackcurrant ice-
   cream sauce 225
chicory 63–5, 66, 97–9, 146
chilli 31, 41, 46, 51, 66, 121–2,
   214, 233
   vodka 248
chives 64, 146, 170, 171, 183
chlodnik 223–5
choy sum 66, 92
chrysanthemum greens 103,
   171, 191
chutney 211–12
cloches 57
clover 42, 43, 45, 130, 171
cocktails 247–8
cold frames 24, 52, 57
comfrey fertiliser 40–2
companion planting 116–18
compost 32–3, 36–42, 45, 46–9
containers 20–3, 30–3, 45, 83,
   95–7, 153–4
cordons 151–3
   step-over 155
coriander 32, 56, 57, 146, 148,
   149
corn salad (lamb's lettuce) 57,
   113–14, 191
cornflower 171, 180
cottage gardens 9
courgette 9, 19, 32, 41, 51, 109,
   124–6, 196, 226
   cake 228
   design ideas 62, 66, 67
   with Pecorino cheese and
     basil on pasta 231–3
   spacing issues 21, 23
crabapple 153, 196, 198
   spiced vodka 247

crocus 169, 170
cropping 54–6
cross-pollination 191, 192
cucumber 24, 30–2, 40–1, 46, 51,
   129–30, 196, 207–8, 223–5
cucumber mosaic virus 130
currants 20, 56, 133, 153, 214
   see also specific currants
cut-and-come-again crops 51,
   106, 138, 192

D
daffodil 169, 171
daisies 171
damson 29, 196, 203–5, 212
   vodka 247
design 60–9, 77, 130
   colour 64–7
   contrast 65–7
dill 10, 51, 60, 148, 179–80, 234
   sour pickles 207–8
diseases 10, 53–4, 57
   see also specific diseases
drifts 21–3
drought 53
drying produce 212

E
earthworms 30, 36
echinacea 244
edible landscaping 9–10, 19–23
espaliers 153, 154

F
F1 hybrids 188, 196
fennel 148, 234, 244
fermentation, wild 236–8
fertiliser 38, 40–2, 48
feverfew 66, 147, 243
field beans 42–3
fig 24, 151, 153, 156–7
flea beetle 92
flowers 166–83
   cut 173–83
   edible 170–3, 244, 246
foraging 25, 26–9
forest gardening 133
freezing produce 211–14
French bean 23, 51, 54, 62, 76–9,
   192, 196, 225

frost pockets 25
fruit trees 19–20, 25, 53
   see also specific trees

G
garlic 66, 84–6, 171, 181, 188,
   233, 244
garlic chives 64, 139
germination 48, 186–7
gherkin 129, 207–8
giant (tree) spinach 90–2
gin, sloe 247–8
globe artichoke 66, 67, 136, 169,
   181
gluts 23, 54, 124
gooseberry 151–4, 162, 196, 214
granny's bonnet 171
grape hyacinth 169
gratin, Jerusalem artichoke 231
grazing rye 44, 45
green manures 42–5
   deep fibrous-rooted 42, 44, 45
   nitrogen-fixing 42–3, 45
   quick growing 42, 43–4, 45
growbags 30
gundru 238

H
hardening off 52
harvest 25, 196–215
hawthorn 26, 29
hellebore 180
herbal teas 240–7
herbs 146–51, 183, 214
heritage varieties 188
Himalayan balsam 234
hollyhock 171
honeyberry 163
horseradish 29, 32, 139–41
humus 36
hungry gap 25, 29
hyssop 166, 244, 247

I
ice plant 168, 176–9
ice-cream
   blackcurrant and chestnut
     sauce 225
   raspberry jam 225

J

jams/jellies 196–205, 225
Japanese knotweed spears 221
Jekyll, Gertrude 21
Jerusalem artichoke 25, 136–8
    gratin 231
    soufflé 230–1

K

kale 25, 31, 46, 51, 56, 66, 67,
    87–9, 133, 176, 180, 192, 233,
    237–8
kiwi 23, 153
kohl rabi 49, 54, 66, 89

L

ladybirds 76
land cress 31, 57, 66, 110–13,
    191
lavender 24, 147–8, 183, 233,
    243–4
    biscuits 222–3
leaching 42, 43
leafmould 33
leek 41, 66, 90, 228
lemon balm 66, 133, 243, 244
lemon grass 243, 244
lemon verbena 243, 244
lettuce 9, 19–21, 23, 32, 45,
    106–10, 225
    cut-and-come-again 51, 106,
        138
    cropping/harvest 54, 56, 109
    design ideas 64, 66, 67
    flower combinations 169, 179
    hearting 106
    protection 57, 110
    seeds 48–9, 51, 106–9, 191–2
Leyland cypress 19
linden flowers 246
liqueurs 247–8
local environments 12
loganberry 160, 196
lovage 66, 148, 234

M

magnolia 19
mangetout 65, 72, 75
marigold (calendula) 9, 10, 31,
    51, 95, 118, 130, 171, 173–6,
    244

marrow 124
Mexican ground cherry 65, 122
mibuna 92
mice 75–6
microgreens 148, 192
mildew 130
minestrone soup 225–6
mint 32, 65, 66, 147, 149, 159,
    240, 243–4
mipoona 92
mitsuba 144, 146
mizuna 92, 207
mulberry 153
mulches 45, 133–6, 156, 166–8
mushrooms 26, 29
mustards 31, 43–5, 56, 66, 92–3,
    95, 207, 222, 233
myoga 146

N

nasturtium 31, 51, 77, 171, 225
nectarine 151, 153, 154
nettle 25, 29, 42
    soup 218–21
nigella 51, 87, 95, 168, 179, 181,
    233
nitrogen 38, 40, 42
    -fixation 42–3, 45
noodles, instant, with chard,
    garlic and hot pepper 233

O

olive 154, 243, 244
onion 66, 99
    bunching 32, 114
    ornamental 170
    perennial 141
orache 66, 90
oregano/marjoram 64, 147–8,
    181, 183
    Cuban 149
    golden 31, 64, 66
oregon grape jam 205
oriental greens 57, 66, 92–3,
    171, 222
oswega tea 243

P

pak choi 66, 92
pansy 31, 51

parsley 31–2, 56, 64, 139, 146,
    226, 228
parsnip 9, 51, 67, 93–5, 168
pasta, courgette, with Pecorino
    cheese and basil 231–3
paths, keyhole 64
peach 23, 151, 153, 154
pear 153, 154, 155, 156, 196
peas 32, 43, 51, 66, 72–5, 88,
    191, 192
peat 36
pectin 196–8
pepper 46, 48, 51, 66
perilla 32, 51, 149
permaculture 16–19
pesticides 29, 170
pests 10, 21–3, 45, 53–4
    see also specific pests
phosphorus 38, 40
pickles 205–12
    bread and butter 208, 210
    one-night 205–6
    Soil Sisters 210–11
pinks 171, 176
plug-plants 46
plum 154–5, 196, 212
poisonous plants 29
pollution 29
polyculture 9–12
polytunnels 57
pomegranate 153
poppy 51, 95, 168, 191, 234
potagers 9, 62
potassium 38, 40, 41
potato 10–12, 45, 65, 95–7, 218,
    225–6, 228
potato blight 97
preserving 196–214
pricking out 49–51
propagators 48, 51
protecting plants 57
pruning 116
pumpkin 23, 126–8, 214, 234
purslane 113

Q

quince 19, 153, 156

R

rabbits 156
raddichio (red chicory) 97–9

radish 9–10, 20–1, 45, 49, 51, 54, 56–7, 67, 93, 114–15, 138, 207, 223–5
raspberry 20, 29, 133, 151, 159, 196, 214, 243
  jam 203
  jam ice-cream 225
  leaf tea 246
recipes 218–38
redcurrant 155, 162, 196
rhubarb 65–6, 133, 136, 144–6, 196
rocket 10, 57, 113, 148, 171, 191, 233
rogueing 191, 192
roots 29
rose 171, 243
rosehips 243, 246–7
rosemary 24, 147, 148, 170, 183, 240, 243, 244
rowan jelly 195
runner bean 51, 79, 192, 196
runners 159
rust 90

S

sage 66, 147, 170, 171, 176, 183, 243, 244
  purple 169, 176, 181
salad leaves 25, 29, 57, 66–7, 106–15, 138
salad Nicoise 225
salsola (land seaweed) 51, 103
sauerkraut 236–8
scafata 221–2
scilla 169
sedum 168, 176–9
seedlings 49–52
seeds 46–9, 168, 186–93
  edible 233–4
  germination 48, 186–7
  saving/storage 186, 188–91
  sowing 46–9, 51
shallot 99, 225
sizes of plants 67–9
sloe gin 247–8
Slow Food movement 133
slugs and snails 23, 49, 79, 83–4, 88, 97, 108, 110, 130, 168, 179
  control 54

soil 19, 32
  organic matter 34–7
  types 36–7
Soil Sisters 210–11, 236
sorrel 149
soufflés, Jerusalem artichoke 230–1
soup 218–21, 223–5, 225–8
spacing 20–1, 23–5
spinach 31, 51, 57, 233
stepping stones 64
stevia 244
stews 221–2
straight line gardening 62
strawberry 26, 31–2, 56, 64, 130, 133, 138, 151, 154, 157–9, 169, 198
sugar 198
sugar snap peas 72, 75
summer squash *see* courgette
sunberry 160
sunflower 25, 51, 67, 77, 118, 126, 166, 168, 179, 234
suntraps 23–4
supports 75
sustainability 26, 32–3
sweet cicely 65, 149–51
sweetcorn 9, 23, 25, 51, 60, 65, 123–4, 126
Swiss chard 31, 51, 56, 66, 88, 99–103, 179–80, 233, 237–8

T

tatsoi 92
tayberry 160
teas, herbal 240–7
Three Sisters 9
thyme 24, 32, 64, 66–7, 138, 147–8, 169, 183, 243–4, 246
tomatillo 122
tomato 10, 24, 66, 115–21, 188, 196
  bush/cordon 115–116
  container grown 30–2, 45
  feeding 40–1
  green chutney 211–12
  recipes 221, 226
  seeds 46, 48–9, 51, 116
tomato blight 121
topsoil 32, 34

trees 19–20
  see also specific trees
tulip 169–70
turnip 207

V

valerian 65, 169, 176
Verbena bonariensis 176, 180
vine 24, 151, 153, 154
viola 31, 51, 87, 89, 130, 173, 181, 191
violet 171
vodka
  chilli 248
  damson 247
  spiced crabapple 247

W

walls 23
watering 33, 51, 53, 118, 156
weeds 52, 136
  perennial 38–40, 52
whisky, blackberry 247
white currant 162
wind 25
wineberry 160
winter greens 24, 25
winter savory 147, 148, 183, 243, 246
winter squash 66, 126–8, 214
winter tares 42, 43

This book is published to accompany the television series entitled *The Edible Garden*, first broadcast on BBC2 in 2010.

Executive Producer: Gill Tierney

3 5 7 9 10 8 6 4 2

Published in 2010 by BBC Books, an imprint of Ebury Publishing.
A Random House Group Company

p.225 Blackcurrant and chestnut ice-cream sauce adapted from *Fruit in Season* by Marian Denny (Penguin, 1979); p.221 Scafata adapted from *Verdura: Vegetables Italian Style* by Viana La Place (William Morrow, 1991)

The Random House Group Limited Reg. No. 954009

Addresses for companies within the Random House Group can be found at
www.randomhouse.co.uk

A CIP catalogue record for this book is available from the British Library.

ISBN 978 1 84 607974 0

Mixed Sources
Product group from well-managed
forests and other controlled sources
www.fsc.org Cert no. SGS-COC-005091
© 1996 Forest Stewardship Council
FSC

The Random House Group Limited supports the Forest Stewardship Council (FSC), the leading international forest certification organisation. All our titles that are printed on Greenpeace approved FSC certified paper carry the FSC logo. Our paper procurement policy can be found at www.rbooks.co.uk/environment

Commissioning editor: Lorna Russell
Project editor: Caroline McArthur
Copy-editor: Charlie Ryrie
Designer: Two Associates
Photographer: Simon Wheeler
Production: David Brimble

Colour origination by: XY Digital
Printed and bound in the UK by Butler, Tanner and Dennis Ltd

To buy books by your favourite authors and register for offers, visit www.rbooks.co.uk